# In Defense of Juveniles Sentenced to Life

This book examines how attorneys enable a meaningful opportunity for release for individuals sentenced to life as juveniles. The work provides a detailed overview of how legal representation facilitates opportunities for release for juveniles sentenced to life: "juvenile lifers". It contributes to the broader literature on the importance of legal representation in the criminal legal system by investigating the role of an attorney in the parole process. Drawing on interviews with lawyers and qualitative content analyses of attorney participation in parole recordings from one state, the study illustrates how attorney assistance provides an important due process protection in the highly discretionary context of parole. The analysis of attorney representation is situated in the history of how they became prominent in the criminal legal system, and how their assistance has been viewed as vital in the parole process. Prior criminological and legal research relates the impact a lawyer can have by preparing a juvenile lifer candidate to present a suitable narrative for release, one that relates their diminished criminal culpability and rehabilitative efforts to prepare for life beyond prison.

The work will be relevant to students, academics, and policy makers, particularly for state parole boards, public defender agencies, and legislatures. While the analysis is based on the experience of one state, the findings are generalizable to other states and countries that similarly conduct parole board hearings for not just their juvenile populations but also adults.

**Stuti S. Kokkalera** is an Assistant Professor in the Department of Criminal Justice and Criminology, College of Criminal Justice, Sam Houston State University, USA.

**Routledge Contemporary Issues in Criminal Justice and Procedure**
Series Editor Ed Johnston *is a Senior Lecturer in Law, Bristol Law School, University of the West of England (UWE), UK.*

**The Law of Disclosure**
A Perennial Problem in Criminal Justice
*Edited by Ed Johnston and Tom Smith*

**Challenges in Criminal Justice**
*Edited by Ed Johnston*

**Probation, Mental Health and Criminal Justice**
Towards Equivalence
*Edited by Charlie Brooker and Coral Sirdifield*

**In Defense of Juveniles Sentenced to Life**
Legal Representation and Juvenile Criminal Justice
*Stuti S. Kokkalera*

**Fair Trial Rules of Evidence**
The Case Law of the European Court of Human Rights
*Jurkka Jämsä*

See more at www.routledge.com/Routledge-Research-in-Legal-History/book-series/CONTEMPCJP

# In Defense of Juveniles Sentenced to Life

Legal Representation and Juvenile Criminal Justice

**Stuti S. Kokkalera**

Routledge
Taylor & Francis Group

LONDON AND NEW YORK

First published 2022
by Routledge
4 Park Square, Milton Park, Abingdon, Oxon OX14 4RN

and by Routledge
605 Third Avenue, New York, NY 10158

*Routledge is an imprint of the Taylor & Francis Group, an informa business*

*British Library Cataloguing-in-Publication Data*
A catalogue record for this book is available from the British Library

*Library of Congress Cataloging-in-Publication Data*
A catalog record for this book has been requested

ISBN: 978-1-032-05299-1 (hbk)
ISBN: 978-1-032-05302-8 (pbk)
ISBN: 978-1-003-19691-4 (ebk)

DOI: 10.4324/9781003196914

Typeset in Times New Roman
by Apex CoVantage, LLC

# Contents

# Acknowledgments

This manuscript stems primarily from my doctoral work. I owe my deepest gratitude to Dr. Simon Singer, my dissertation committee chair. Simon provided multiple rounds of feedback on each chapter, and his insight into juvenile lifers made so much of this work possible. I am also grateful to my other dissertation committee members who provided feedback on earlier versions of this manuscript: former Chief Justice (Dr.) Roderick Ireland and Dr. Jacob Stowell.

I very much appreciate all the attorneys who agreed to be interviewed. Their generosity with their time and openness with sharing their experiences made this study and this manuscript possible. I am in awe of all that these attorneys do for their juvenile lifer clients. This book is dedicated to all those attorneys who show up every day in defense of our youth.

A big thank you to series editor, Dr. Ed Johnston, for the feedback, support, and encouragement in writing this manuscript, as well as the editorial team at Routledge.

I also want to extend my gratitude to my weekly writing group: Katie, Javier, John, Jared, Andia, Jonathan, and Cassy! Thank you for the motivation and feedback.

I am eternally grateful to my parents Subbaiah and Shubha, my husband Ganesh, as well as our pup for life, Kirby. They checked in with me whenever I tried to check out of writing—thank you.

# Table of Abbreviations

| Abbreviation | Full Explanation |
|---|---|
| AA | Alcoholics Anonymous |
| ABA | American Bar Association |
| ACLU | American Civil Liberties Union |
| AP | Associated Press |
| LWOP | Life without the possibility of parole |
| NA | Narcotics Anonymous |
| NJDC | National Juvenile Defender Center |
| PCP | Phencyclidine (or Angel Dust) |

# Table of Cases

# Table of Legislation

# Introduction

## In Defense of Youth

In the early years of his childhood, Michael lost his mother to a drug over-dose. His father soon abandoned him and his four siblings, forcing him to move in with his grandmother and uncle. His grandmother, also drug-addicted, was distant and neglectful, while his uncle was physically and emotionally abusive. State welfare officials became involved, and Michael and his siblings were removed from the custody of their grandmother and uncle. Separated from his siblings, Michael ended up in foster care, con-stantly shifting between group homes. By the time Michael turned 16, he had already come to the attention of the juvenile court for truancy and alco-hol abuse.

One day in the fall of 1979, 16-year-old Michael and his friend were hanging out after consuming alcohol and angel dust (PCP), a hallucinogen. Michael's 17-year-old friend suggested that they should "assault someone" and he agreed. While walking around their neighborhood intoxicated, they came upon Jane Smith.[1] Michael knew Jane from one of his foster homes and did not get along with her. She had previously reported Michael's messy room to their foster care guardians and used him as an excuse to run away. His friend too knew Jane and considered her to be an easy target due to her familiarity with them.

Michael and his friend asked Jane for help as a lookout for a robbery, and she agreed. Instead of the robbery, they led her to a shed in a secluded spot where the two teenagers sexually assaulted her. Michael's friend subse-quently stabbed her to death. Following his arrest, Michael entered a guilty plea to the charges of rape and second-degree murder. He was sentenced to life with the possibility of parole after a minimum of 15 years. He was also the prosecution's main witness against his friend, who was convicted for first-degree murder and sentenced to life without parole (hereafter "LWOP") at the age of 17.

DOI: 10.4324/9781003196914-1

Despite receiving a parole-eligible life sentence, Michael has been incarcerated since his conviction in 1981. He has 14 disciplinary infractions throughout the course of his imprisonment, all for non-violent reasons. He has engaged in the sex offender treatment program, received his GED certificate, participates in weekly Alcoholics Anonymous/Narcotics Anonymous (AA/NA) meetings, and is employed at his prison. Still, Michael has been denied release following four different parole hearings.

Michael may never be released on parole because his crime is too horrific. At his latest parole board hearing in 2012, when pressed by the parole board to relate why he attacked Jane, Michael stated that he viewed her impending assault as an act of revenge for the way she treated him when they were living together in the same group home. In the written decision produced by the parole board denying release, Michael is described as "a destructive force in his community prior to his incarceration". The parole board is also concerned with a diagnosis of "psychopathic personality disorder" that Michael received when he was newly incarcerated as an adolescent—a characterological label that is no longer appropriate for individuals who are in early stages of adolescent development (Grisso & Kavanaugh, 2016). The denial of parole is further justified by Michael's lack of social support in the community. At his hearing, Michael informs the parole board that he is no longer in contact with his siblings, and that his uncle who once victimized him would be willing to help him in his reentry. Crucially, Michael appeared by himself without counsel for his parole hearings, and despite his middle-aged appearance, he does not confidently relate his preparation for release from incarceration.

Michael is one of the estimated nearly 10,000 individuals serving life sentences they received as teenagers, referred to generally as juvenile lifers (ACLU, 2016; Nellis & King, 2009; Nellis, 2012, 2017).[2] About a third of that juvenile lifer population includes those who received LWOP terms for their crimes (see Associated Press, 2017). In 2010, the U.S. Supreme Court (hereafter "the Supreme Court") banned LWOP for juveniles convicted of non-homicide offenses, directing states to provide a "meaningful opportunity for release based on demonstrated maturity and rehabilitation" (*Graham v. Florida*, 2010, p. 75). In the *Graham* decision (2010), the Supreme Court identified state parole boards as the appropriate forum for a meaningful opportunity for release because it is the "most established and regularized mechanism for back-end sentencing" (Bierschbach, 2012, p. 1780). Two years later, in *Miller v. Alabama* (2012), the Supreme Court banned mandatory LWOP for juveniles. In *Montgomery v. Louisiana* (2016, p. 736), the Supreme Court clarified that *Miller* (2012) applied retroactively, meaning that juvenile lifers serving automatic LWOP terms are eligible for release which could be in the form of a parole board hearing.

States have grappled with how to provide their juveniles a meaningful opportunity for release. As of May 2021, 25 states and the District of Columbia have replaced LWOP terms with parole eligible life sentences (Rovner, 2021). Some states have retained the option of a discretionary LWOP sentence and others have banned all LWOP terms altogether (Rovner, 2014). In the state examined in this book,[3] the highest appellate court determined that the parole board is an appropriate avenue to undo juvenile LWOP terms because the state agency has been tasked with determining early release for juvenile lifers with parole eligible life sentences, like Michael.

What is it about parole that qualifies it as providing a meaningful opportunity for release? The state's highest appellate court decision noted that it is within the parole board's purview to evaluate the circumstances surrounding the crime including the age of the candidate at the time, as well as relevant information from the years of incarceration.[4] The place where the parole board makes judgements of release suitability is a formal, administrative hearing with the candidate. The parole board hearing can be viewed as a "performative space" where interpersonal interactions shape other's opinions of oneself (Goffman, 1959). A parole board hearing features ritualized interactions between parole board members, the candidate, and other participants like opposers and supporters of release. Though parole members are familiar with case details that include criminal records as well as rehabilitative efforts in prison, the hearing is an avenue for the candidate to weave a convincing narrative that explains the motives for their crime, their remorse and personal growth (Radelet & Roberts, 1983).

Importantly, a candidate's presentation at the hearing can be enhanced through the assistance of counsel because attorneys are well-positioned to assist parole candidates with presenting a credible defense of their character after decades of incarceration (Aviram, 2020; Russell, 2014, 2016; Thomas & Reingold, 2017). Among the population of candidates appearing for parole, juvenile lifers a particularly vulnerable segment. A juvenile lifer's age at time of offense may be viewed as a cognitive deficit that impacts decision-making capacities (Cohen, 1965). Juvenile lifers may also suffer from mental health issues. Some, like Michael, no longer have familial support in the community. Most have experienced violence as children and adolescents which not only contextualizes the reasons for their offense but has also impacted their adjustment to prison life (Nellis, 2012). While there is hope for release through the Supreme Court's rulings, there are no guarantees because parole boards have enormous discretionary power with limited judicial oversight and minimal due process protections (ACLU, 2016; Ball, 2011).

State and federal courts have generally been reluctant to raise the levels of due process protections in parole board hearings to avoid judicial scrutiny

(Newman, 1972). For instance, three Supreme Court decisions in the 1970s reiterated that granting all due process protections would change the discretionary nature of parole systems. In *Morrissey v. Brewer* (1972, p. 482), the Supreme Court found that only in a revocation of parole was "some orderly process, however informal" necessary. A year later, the Supreme Court found that an individual facing the possibility of parole can be afforded legal representation, determined on a case-by-case basis (*Gagnon v. Scarpelli*, 1973). Finally, in *Greenholtz v. Inmates of the Nebraska Penal and Correctional Complex* (1979), the Supreme Court clarified that when a state's parole statute creates a "protectible expectation of parole" only then a minimal standard of due process would apply, including the right to counsel.[5] This meant that it was up to states to legislate if parole candidates have access to legal assistance (Annitto, 2014; Bierschbach, 2012).

Therefore, even if states have opted to provide parole hearings to juvenile lifers, the assistance of counsel is not guaranteed. The state examined in this book is one among a handful of states to recognize the right to counsel at an initial parole board hearing for juvenile lifers following the Supreme Court's decisions.[6] In 2015, the state's highest state appellate court, clarified that juvenile lifers who were previously sentenced to LWOP have the right to legal representation at their initial parole hearing, state funds for calling expert witnesses and a limited appeal against the parole board's denial. The highest appellate court characterized legal representation as integral to facilitating a meaningful opportunity for release because a parole hearing "involves complex and multifaceted issues that require the potential marshalling, presentation, and rebuttal of information derived from many sources".[7] The right to counsel was extended to parole-eligible juvenile lifers in a subsequent decision that same year. While the court's decision noted that it assumes the right to counsel for juvenile lifers to extend to initial hearings, it declined to discuss whether it would apply to other hearings or other parole candidates. Prior to these decisions, parole-eligible juvenile lifers did not have a guaranteed right to counsel but could hire an attorney if they could afford to, request representation through a legal aid clinic or seek pro bono services of law firms. So, juvenile lifer parole candidates like Michael who required assistance were not guaranteed legal representation, even if they were indigent.

Michael's story is one of many that constitutes a vulnerable segment of the incarcerated population. His case confirms the need for legal representation in a hearing that insists on candid remarks about the worst experiences of a juvenile lifer's life. The developmental status of juvenile lifers, impacted by traumatic events and decades of incarceration, suggests that not all are equally capable of advocating for themselves and should be afforded the assistance of counsel (Simkins & Cohen, 2015). The Supreme

Court's directive of a meaningful opportunity leaves it up to states to determine what that should entail, including if there is a need for the assistance of counsel in the parole process. Indeed, while a parole board hearing is not a trial, it seemingly proceeds like one. The rules of evidence and the burden of proof are less clear. The jurisprudential recognition of the importance of attorneys presents a compelling question: how does legal representation enable a meaningful opportunity for release for juvenile lifer parole candidates?

**Chapter 1** provides an overview of the Supreme Court's vision for a meaningful opportunity for release and state attempts to comply with the jurisprudential mandate of recognizing a juvenile lifer's adolescence as a reason to mitigate culpability and acknowledge rehabilitative efforts. **Chapter 2** relates how the presence of counsel has evolved in the parole process, by drawing on the Supreme Court's interpretation of the right to an attorney per the Sixth Amendment to the Constitution. The historical lens is important to illustrate the conflict between procedural formality in guaranteeing due process protections in administrative settings like parole and the substantive goals of parole boards. **Chapter 3** next elaborates on how legal representation can enable a meaningful opportunity for release by keeping up with the standards of effective representation. How attorneys provide effective representation is associated with the type of resources available. In the context of parole, attorneys are further expected to draw on the candidate's adolescence at the time of the crime to make the case for their release. **Chapter 4** details the study setting, data sources (interviews with attorneys and parole board recordings) and methods of analysis. Qualitative coding methods including content analysis and discourse analytical techniques were employed to examine how attorneys operate in the parole process. **Chapter 5** presents findings from the qualitative analyses, revealing how attorneys can enable and enhance a meaningful opportunity for release for juvenile lifers. Finally, **Chapter 6** situates the findings related to attorney assistance in the parole process for juvenile lifers in the broader literature on the relevance of the right to legal representation in criminal justice proceedings.

## Notes

1 Name withheld to protect identity of victim.
2 A more humanizing term is "individuals incarcerated as adolescents", but this population specifically refers to those who received life terms before they reached age of majority, i.e., 18 years old.
3 The state has been de-identified due to ongoing projects and to protect the identity of parole candidates, board members and attorneys who were interviewed.
4 Decision is available upon request.

5  The wording of the Nebraska statute (Neb.Rev.Stat. § 83–1,107(1)(b) [1976]) created an expectation of parole rather than a hope of release by using the words "shall grant parole" (DBH, 1980).
6  An initial hearing is the first parole board hearing that is scheduled after serving the specified minimum term of a life sentence, anywhere between 15 and 30 years depending on the type of crime.
7  Decision is available upon request.

# 1 The Meaning of a Meaningful Opportunity

## The Supreme Court's View of Juvenile Lifers

Over the last 15 years, the Supreme Court has altered the legal landscape on the sentencing of juveniles (Moriearty, 2017a, 2017b). The Eighth Amendment to the U.S. Constitution precludes "cruel and unusual punishment" which implies a ban on abhorrent punishments like physical torture and sentencing terms that are excessive to the crime committed (Hoesterey, 2017).[1] Through three decisions, the Supreme Court has expanded the protections of the Eighth Amendment to juveniles convicted of the most serious offences, recognizing that children are different from adults (Feld, 2017).

First, in *Roper v. Simmons* (2005) the Supreme Court was confronted with the question of whether the death penalty applied to adolescents younger than 18.[2] Previously in *Thompson v. Oklahoma* (1988), the Supreme Court had barred the execution of youth who were aged 15 and younger. A year later, the same Court upheld the use of the death sentence for youth aged 16 or 17 years old if they were convicted of a capital offense (*Stanford v. Kentucky*, 1989). More than a decade later, in *Roper*, a majority of five justices turned to the "evolving standards of decency test" to conclude that it was cruel and unusual to sentence a teenager younger than 18 to death. Justice Kennedy's majority opinion pointed out that a national consensus had emerged with states banning the death penalty altogether or its use against juveniles aged seventeen and younger. The majority further cited socio-scientific research to support the ban on the death penalty for adolescents. Specifically, three characteristics distinguished adolescents from adults even in the most serious cases: (1) their lack of maturity and an underdeveloped sense of responsibility; (2) their susceptibility to negative influences and peer pressure; and (3) their transitory personalities (*Roper*, 2005, pp. 569–570).

Five years later in *Graham v. Florida* (2010), the Supreme Court was confronted with the question of whether an LWOP sentence was

DOI: 10.4324/9781003196914-2

unconstitutional when applied to minors convicted of non-homicide offenses such as armed robbery or rape.[3] Relying on its prior decision in *Roper* (2005), the majority in *Graham* found that the lesser culpability of children and adolescents precludes courts from sentencing them to die in prison for a non-homicide offense (Drinan, 2012; Moriearty, 2017a). The decision did not prohibit states from sentencing their juveniles to life, but it barred them from concluding that all juveniles are incapable of reform. Due to an adolescent's heightened capacity for reform, states must provide "some meaningful opportunity to obtain release based on demonstrated maturity and rehabilitation" (*Graham*, 2010, p. 75). The hope for release is predicated on a state's prerogative to "explore the means and mechanisms for compliance" (*Graham*, 2010, p. 75). Justice Thomas' dissent in *Graham* (2010) predicted that defining the criteria for a meaningful opportunity would plague states including who benefits from the decision, whether it is retroactively applicable, and whether it applies to juveniles serving other long-term parole eligible sentences (Drinan, 2012).

Shortly after *Graham* (2010), a narrowly split Supreme Court prohibited the use of mandatory LWOP sentences for juveniles convicted of homicide offenses in *Miller v. Alabama* (2012).[4] In its reasoning, the Supreme Court relied on previous decisions that directed sentencing courts to consider the mitigating characteristics of defendants before sentencing them to death (*Woodson v. North Carolina*, 1976; *Lockett v. Ohio*, 1978). Justice Elena Kagan's majority opinion reiterated the findings in *Roper* (2005) and *Graham* (2010) to emphasize that the Eighth Amendment forbids a sentencing scheme that does not provide a meaningful opportunity to obtain release. Mandatory terms preclude the consideration of chronological age which suggests hallmark features of adolescence such as impulsivity, immaturity, and a failure to appreciate risks. A mandatory term further disregards a juvenile's personal biography including:

> family and home environment that surrounds him—and from which he cannot usually extricate himself—no matter how brutal or dysfunctional . . . [and] the circumstances of the homicide offense, including the extent of his participation in the conduct and the way familial and peer pressures may have affected him . . . ignores that he might have been charged and convicted of a lesser offense if not for incompetencies associated with youth . . . and finally, this mandatory punishment disregards the possibility of rehabilitation.
>
> (*Miller*, 2012, p. 478)

A meaningful opportunity, therefore, should entail the consideration of five *Miller* factors: (1) immaturity or impetuosity, and failure to appreciate risks;

(2) family and home environment; (3) extent of participation in the crime including any peer pressure; (4) inability to assist in their own legal defense; and (5) the possibility of rehabilitation (Levick & Schwartz, 2013; Marshall, 2019, p. 1643).

However, in banning only automatic LWOP, the *Miller* Court emphasized that states have the authority to determine appropriate sentencing terms but *may not* presume that *all* juveniles are irreparably corrupt without giving an opportunity to present their mitigated culpability and potential for reform (*own emphasis*). In other words, the decision did not foreclose the possibility of judges sentencing a juvenile to LWOP if the evidence suggests that a youth is irreparably corrupt, even if such a characterization conflicts with social scientific evidence of the transiency of adolescence (Crawford-Pechukas, 2019).

Post-*Miller*, states diverged not only in terms of how to undo their automatic LWOP provisions but also if the decision to provide a meaningful opportunity should extend to those juveniles previously sentenced to LWOP (Rovner, 2014). In *Montgomery v. Louisiana* (2016), the Supreme Court clarified that a meaningful opportunity applies to juveniles already serving a LWOP sentence.[5] Citing Wyoming's statutory provision for parole eligibility as an example, the Supreme Court noted that states may "remedy a *Miller* violation by permitting juvenile homicide offenders to be considered for parole, rather than by resentencing them" (*Montgomery*, 2016, p. 736). States are now required to provide some form of discretionary release through resentencing and/or parole hearings (Drinan, 2017; Kokkalera & Singer, 2019). Though *Miller* (2012) and *Montgomery* (2016) directly addressed about 2,500 individuals across the country who were sentenced as juveniles to LWOP (AP, 2017; Rovner, 2014, 2017), their potential impact is on a larger population of juveniles sentenced to life with the possibility of parole (Nellis, 2017; Nellis & King, 2009) and even larger proportion of youths serving long sentences of less than life.[6]

In 2021, a majority of six justices held that *Miller* (2012) and *Montgomery* (2016) did not require a sentencing (or resentencing) authority to make a separate factual finding of permanent incorrigibility before imposing an LWOP sentence for a juvenile defendant (*Jones v. Mississippi*, 2021).[7] According to the majority, there is no prerequisite for judges to provide detailed reasons of a juvenile defendant or juvenile lifer's incapacity to rehabilitate when justifying an LWOP term. The dissenting justices noted that the majority "gutted" *Miller* and *Montgomery* because it allows judges to "never determine, even implicitly, whether a juvenile convicted of homicide is one of those rare children whose crimes reflect irreparable corruption" (*Jones*, 2021, p. 1328). Indeed, the week after the *Jones* (2021) decision came down, Evan Miller of *Miller v. Alabama* was resentenced to LWOP

(Faulk, 2021b). Miller's resentencing hearing first occurred in 2017, and the judge noted that he was "reviewing ongoing developments in the caselaw that continue to provide insight as to the law that must guide the decision" (Faulk, 2021). As noted by Justice Sotomayor in the Jones dissent, the Court "reduces *Miller* to a decision requiring just a discretionary sentencing procedure where youth is considered" (*Jones*, 2021, p. 1328).

Importantly, the *Jones* decision (2021) reiterates a state's authority and capacity to either retain or undo juvenile LWOP sentencing. As reminded by Justice Sotomayor, if the goal is to simply provide a chance of release, the Supreme Court would have simply said so. By adding the word "meaningful", the implication is that it is more than just a shot at release—under *Miller*, juveniles "must be given the opportunity to show their crime did not reflect irreparable corruption; and, if it did not, their hope for some years of life outside prison walls must be restored" (*Jones*, 2021, p. 1330).

## Defining a Meaningful Opportunity

Both *Graham* (2010) and *Miller* (2012) refer to a "meaningful opportunity to obtain release". A meaningful opportunity should involve three components: (1) a chance of release at a meaningful point in time; (2) a realistic possibility of release for those who show rehabilitation; and (3) a meaningful opportunity to be heard (Russell, 2014). States have overwhelmingly focused on determining what would be a meaningful point in time to determine release, ranging from 15 years to serving 51 years of a life sentence before coming up for parole (Rovner, 2014, 2017). In conjunction with defining a minimum term, criminal law provisions in 25 states and the District of Columbia have incorporated "*Miller* factors" that explicitly recognize adolescence as a mitigating factor in sentencing (Feld, 2017). In general, states have looked to the *Miller* decision as requiring individualized sentencing hearings for juveniles convicted of homicide offenses (Fiorillo, 2013). At present, 25 states and the District of Columbia have banned juvenile LWOP; four states do not have any juvenile lifers with LWOP terms (Rovner, 2021). Some states like the one examined in this study went a step further to hold that *Miller* (2012) would apply retroactively. Since the *Montgomery* (2016) decision, other states that did not clarify retroactivity had to also choose between resentencing and parole board hearings (Kokkalera & Singer, 2019).

## How Is Parole a Meaningful Opportunity for Release?

Parole was introduced in the U.S. in the late 19th century as a reward for good conduct in the correctional institution irrespective of why the individual was incarcerated in the first place (Witmer, 1925, 1927). If a parole candidate could show that they abided by the rules of the institution and availed programs necessary to rehabilitate themselves, they could leave the institution with certain rules in place with oversight by correctional authorities for the remainder of their sentence.

Early systems of parole relied on prison authorities to decide release which led to complaints of arbitrary decision-making (Witmer, 1925). In response, states shifted the authority of release to independent parole boards comprised of appointed officials. The motivation for independent parole boards varied—parole was characterized as a humanitarian offering of sentence mitigation; a reward to control in-prison conduct; an economic incentive for states to reduce spending on prisons and for reformers, parole was the rehabilitative ideal that would enable successful reentry (Newman, 1972). Whatever the motive, by 1940, all states had a parole board (Rhine, 2012). The focus of parole boards was to determine if a candidate was ready for community supervision based on a review of correctional officer reports, treatment evidence, no new violations, and a network of supporters (Hier, 1973).

In the later part of the 20th century, rising crime rates particularly among youth received an extraordinary amount of attention from the media (Bishop & Feld, 2014). The political response was swift and emphasized tough on crime approaches (Hagan, 2010). Determinate sentencing that fixed a compulsory mandatory prison term was introduced as a solution to the ills of indeterminate sentencing that allowed for too much discretion especially at the hands of a few parole board members (Palacios, 1994). As a result, states either got rid of parole entirely (Arizona, Florida, Maine) or heavily curtailed their discretionary processes like in Illinois (Ruhland et al., 2017). Despite historical changes and heavy criticism following high-profile cases of those on parole recidivating, parole release remains an influential component of America's correctional landscape and avenue to undo decades of mass incarceration (Clear & Frost, 2014; Reitz & Rhine, 2020). As more states recognize the vitality of parole in reducing their incarcerated populations, there is an increased need to shed light on the discretionary release practices of parole boards.

Discretionary release practices are not couched within the same legal formalities of a criminal court (Ball, 2011; Medwed, 2008; Rhine, 2012). While a minimum term is established for an indeterminate sentence, it is ultimately up to board members to decide if an individual must serve more time before being released (Ball, 2011; Howard, 2017). Decisions can rely on any aspect of a candidate's case including documentation related to earlier stages of the criminal legal system such as arrest reports, trial documents, and post-conviction proceedings (Carroll & Burke, 1990; Hawkins, 1983, 1986; Morgan & Smith, 2005). Parole boards also review prison reports about infractions and rehabilitative programming (Morgan & Smith, 2005; Bernhardt et al., 2010); solicited and unsolicited letters of support and opposition (Proctor, 1999), and risk assessment scores (Harcourt, 2015).

The Supreme Court's directive to provide a meaningful opportunity led to 15 states like the one examined to clarify that juvenile lifers initially sentenced to LWOP were entitled to release after serving a minimum term. The state's highest appellate court further ruled that a parole board hearing would be the avenue for a meaningful opportunity for release since they were already equipped with making decisions for juvenile lifers serving parole-eligible life sentences. As noted by the appellate court, parole boards should conduct a meaningful review that takes into account "the circumstances surrounding the commission of the crime, including the age of the offender, together with all the relevant information pertaining to the offender's character and actions during the intervening years since conviction".[8] Therefore, a meaningful opportunity implies that parole boards are expected to consider a juvenile lifer's adolescence-related reasons for the offense and how those reasons affected their efforts at rehabilitation.

However, existing discretionary release practices may prevent parole boards from fully recognizing adolescence as a reason to mitigate culpability. Recognition of reduced culpability is difficult because a juvenile lifer's status as a misguided teenager is hard to visualize when they are middle-aged adults at the time of their parole board hearing (Boone, 2015). A juvenile lifer candidate is already defined as a criminally responsible adult throughout the criminal legal process (Feld, 2017). Additionally, an offense-based focus is unavoidable because parole boards are statutorily required to consider the severity of the sentencing offense (Ruhland et al., 2017). More horrific the crime, more remote is the possibility of release because the recognition of adolescence in terms of mitigated culpability and rehabilitative efforts may count for less against the nature of the crime.

Discretionary release practices are also impacted by the politics of parole boards since members are usually appointed by state governors. Governors who campaign with a tough on crime message tend to appoint parole board chairpersons oriented towards a more retributionist approach to release decisions (Howard, 2017). Some parole board members may not buy into the role of mitigation at time of offense, particularly if it involved a serious act of violence. Prior research has also shown that parole boards are overly cautious about releasing candidates who committed serious offenses even if they pose a low risk to recidivate (Drinan, 2017; Schwartzapfel, 2015).

Given the highly discretionary nature of parole board hearings and the lack of definitive criteria of how to implement a meaningful opportunity, due process protections are necessary (Russell, 2014). Yet not all states provide the right to counsel in parole board hearings. There is considerable variability in state parole systems which creates an added complication in determining the due process rights for incarcerated persons seeking discretionary release (Newman, 1972). Most states have a parole agency though states may be restricted from conducting hearings due to determinate sentencing schemes for violent offenses (Kokkalera & Singer, 2019). In states that have retained indeterminate sentences, formal parole board hearings are conducted to determine eventual release, though the exact procedures may vary. Whatever the nature, parole hearings are not considered criminal prosecutions for the purposes of the Sixth Amendment's guaranteed right to counsel (Adams, 1994). As a result, states are generally resistant to raising the due process protections in parole, especially the right to counsel.

## Notes

1 Eighth Amendment to the Constitution (1791): "Excessive bail shall not be required, nor excessive fines imposed, nor cruel and unusual punishments inflicted".
2 Seventeen-year-old Christopher Simmons along with two friends plotted to rob and murder the victim. In the end, Christopher and another friend decided to go ahead with the plan. They broke into the victim's home and then drove her to state park, where they threw her off a bridge. She died by drowning. Even though some mitigating factors (age, no prior criminal history) were considered, Simmons was sentenced to death.
3 Terrence Graham was 16 years old when he and two accomplices attempted to rob a restaurant in Jacksonville, Florida. After his arrest, he was charged as an adult for armed burglary and assault. He pled guilty and received a term of probation. While on probation, he was arrested for armed home invasion. Though he denied his involvement, he admitted to violating his terms of probation because he tried to flee from the police. The judge presiding over his hearing sentenced Graham to life in prison without parole.
4 Evan Miller was 14 years old when he and a friend, while intoxicated, robbed their neighbor and then killed him. Both Miller and his friend struck the victim with a baseball bat and then set the victim's trailer on fire, resulting in the victim's death from smoke inhalation and injuries. Miller was subsequently convicted and sentenced to LWOP. His case was joined by Kuntrell Jackson's case, who was also 14 years old. Jackson served as a look-out for his friend, who fatally shot a store clerk, and both fled without any money from the store. Jackson also received an LWOP sentence for his role in the crime.
5 In 1963, Henry Montgomery was 17 years old when he shot and killed a police officer. He was first convicted of murder and sentenced to death, but on appeal the death sentence was annulled. He was re-tried and received an automatic sentence of LWOP.
6 According to Nellis and King (2009), this would be around 6,800 individuals, but this number may be greater since it does not include numbers post-2009 or lengthy mandatory sentences that resemble a life sentence.
7 Fifteen-year-old Brett Jones was convicted of murdering his grandfather. He received an automatic sentence of LWOP.
8 Decision available upon request.

# 2    The Evolving Right to Legal Representation

While parole decision-making is a case of substantive rationality, elements of formal rationality remain to restrict discretionary justice (Lin et al., 2012, p. 351). Formal rationality is reflected in sentencing options that equate the seriousness of the offense to the retributive force of punishment. In the case of juvenile lifers, a state's discretionary release practices may be restricted because culpability has already been decided by the sentencing offense. Formal rationality is further reflected in the fact that the discretion to release is codified in statute and administrative guidelines that emphasize the nature of the offense (Ruhland et al., 2017). Formal rationality is also evident in due process protections. Formal legal rules like providing the right to counsel can conflict with substantive concerns of the parole board to reduce risk to the community. This chapter draws on the history of legal representation in criminal court and its extension to juvenile court to illuminate the tension between substantive and formal rational concerns.

## The Constitutional Right to Counsel

The Supreme Court was first confronted with the question of whether the right to an attorney under the Constitution's Sixth Amendment for criminal proceedings extends to criminal proceedings in state courts in *Powell v. Alabama* (1932).[1] In *Powell*, nine Black youths were accused of raping two white women. Alabama law required the appointment of counsel in capital cases, but the appointed attorneys did not consult with their clients and had little preparation going into trial. The Supreme Court held that the trials denied due process to the defendants because they were not given a reasonable opportunity to gain effective legal assistance. Qualifying the importance of a defense attorney, the decision granted indigent criminal defendants charged with a capital crime the right to state-appointed counsel. According to a majority of the justices, without counsel, "though he

DOI: 10.4324/9781003196914-3

[the defendant] be not guilty, he faces the danger of conviction because he does not know how to establish his innocence" (*Powell*, 1932, p. 68). Subsequently, in *Johnson v. Zerbst* (1938), the Supreme Court ruled that defendants in federal criminal proceedings have the right to an appointed attorney if they could not afford one.

The right to counsel in state criminal proceedings was addressed again in *Gideon v. Wainright* (1963). When Clarence Gideon was charged with a felony in a Florida state court, he requested the appointment of an attorney since he could not afford one. At the time, attorneys could only be appointed for defendants in capital cases and the state denied Gideon's request. Gideon, representing himself, was found guilty and sentenced to five years in state prison. The Florida Supreme Court denied habeas corpus relief and Gideon appealed the decision to the Supreme Court. Relying on its decision in *Powell* (1932), the Supreme Court held that indigent criminal defendants have the right to court-appointed counsel in state criminal proceedings.

*Gideon* (1963) underscored the role of an attorney in ensuring that constitutional rights of individuals are protected when they have been charged with a crime. Later in *Argesinger v. Hamlin* (1972), the Supreme Court further clarified that the Sixth Amendment's right to counsel extended to any criminal prosecution with the possibility of loss of liberty. The *Argesinger* decision did not make a distinction between a misdemeanor and felony in determining if a defendant had the right to an attorney. While the Supreme Court's decisions were far-reaching, the right to counsel was not immediately available to juveniles (Wills, 2017).

## A Juvenile Defendant's Right to Counsel

Juvenile court is an administrative setting that falls squarely in the camp of substantive justice (Lemert, 1986; Singer, 1996). The first juvenile court in 1899 in Cook County, Illinois, was grounded in the concept of parens patriae (Scholssman, 1977; Zimring, 2000, 2005). The origin of the parens patriae doctrine is unclear, though it was part of the Prerogative Regis and applied to children, individuals with intellectual disabilities, and charities (Curtis, 1976).[2] The doctrine, translated as "the state as parent-surrogate" was invoked to protect children from neglectful parents (Feld, 2017). Without a strict conceptual definition, the parens patriae doctrine allowed for unencumbered discretionary power, where juvenile courts could serve as "benevolent parents" without due process protections for the child (Birckhead, 2010).[3] As a result, the informal nature of the juvenile court circumvented questions about a child's competence to stand trial or whether other due process protections were necessary (Feld, 2017).

Starting in the 1960s, there was increased scrutiny of the juvenile court system, resulting in what is now referred to as the "due process revolution" of the Supreme Court (Bernard & Kurlychek, 2010; Feld, 2017). The first of a series of cases involved 16-year-old Morris Kent Jr. The juvenile court judge did not provide a hearing and based primarily on the probation officer's report, waived the jurisdiction of the juvenile court. Kent was transferred to criminal court and subsequently convicted of rape and robbery. Kent won his appeal in the Supreme Court which found that losing the juvenile court's benefits of treatment-oriented dispositions and confidentiality warranted a hearing with due process protections such as the assistance of counsel, access to records and written findings for appellate review (*Kent v. U.S.*, 1966).

Though the *Kent* Court recognized that certain due process protections are necessary for juveniles, it was limited in its applicability. The right to procedural due process, including the right to legal counsel applied only to hearings where a juvenile would be transferred to criminal court. Moreover, since the case was based on a violation of the District of Columbia's Juvenile Court Act, the decision applied only to Washington, D.C. However, by adopting a general line of reasoning based on the actual performance of the juvenile court, and not its good intentions, the decision led to several states changing their laws to avoid an appeal to the Supreme Court (Bernard & Kurlychek, 2010).

*Kent* paved the way for the Supreme Court to decide whether attorneys should be appointed for juveniles facing delinquency proceedings (Stapleton & Teitelbaum, 1972). In the year following *Kent*, the Supreme Court heard the case of Gerald Gault. Fifteen-year-old Gault was arrested for making an obscene phone call to his neighbor. The arresting officer did not give Gault's parents' notice of his arrest nor were they informed of the hearing before the juvenile court judge. There were several other alleged violations including a non-recorded hearing, forced admissions by Gault before the judge and no legal assistance prior to the hearing. Gault's appellate attorney in the Supreme Court argued that these actions by the juvenile court in Gila County, Arizona violated his juvenile client's constitutional rights to due process.

The Supreme Court agreed with Gault and stated that juveniles facing adjudication hearings in delinquency cases have the right to notice of charges filed; the right to counsel; the privilege against self-incrimination and the right to confront any witnesses (*In Re Gault*, 1967).[4] The Supreme Court reasoned:

> a juvenile needs the assistance of counsel to cope with problems of law, to make skilled inquiry into the facts, to insist upon regularity of the

proceedings, and to ascertain whether he has a defense and to prepare and submit it.

(Gault, 1967, p. 36)

Some scholars argued that the adoption of due process rights into the juvenile court would converge the juvenile and criminal justice systems, where incorporating features of the criminal court would result in the loss of the therapeutic structure and function of the juvenile court (Feld, 1999, 2017; Zimring, 2000, 2005). Complicating the expectations of legal representation is the fact that the Supreme Court did not adequately define the role of counsel for juveniles (Corbin, 2015; Fedders, 2010). Justice Fortas' majority opinion in *Gault* predicated the conflict for attorneys where "the child receives the worst of both worlds: that he gets neither the protections accorded to adults, nor the solicitous care and regenerative treatment postulated for children" (*Gault*, 1967, p. 18).

The *Gault* decision also did not address whether attorneys in juvenile court have special ethical responsibilities where attorneys are required to understand the differences between adolescent and adult offending (Fedders, 2010). Additionally, the Supreme Court did not discuss how juvenile defense attorneys would be hired and trained (Wills, 2017). It was up to states to determine budget and resources for juvenile defense attorneys (Mlyenic, 2008). Despite the presumption of the right to counsel, there is no certainty that an attorney will be experienced in representing juveniles (Drinan, 2017).

While the decision in *Gault* (1967) expected a corresponding increase in legal representation, there are no guarantees in terms of access to or the quality of legal services for juvenile defendants (Foxhoven, 2007). Less than 50% of juveniles received assistance of counsel during delinquency proceedings in a majority of states (Feld, 1988, 1991) and many juveniles did not have any attorney representation (Detrick, 1996). A report by the National Juvenile Defender Center (2017) showed that only 11 states provide legal representation for indigent juvenile defendants facing charges in either juvenile or criminal court. State variation in how legal representation is afforded to juvenile defendants including the presumption of indigency and the ability to waive counsel representation can impact the quality of legal assistance (Kokkalera et al., 2021).

Juvenile court judges could transfer youth to criminal courts (as noted in the *Kent* case), but this option was used rather sparingly, confined to only the most serious cases involving older youth (Bishop & Feld, 2014; Feld, 2017; Zimring, 2010). For instance, Michael who was introduced earlier in this book, was transferred to criminal court through a judicial waiver process because his crimes included rape and second-degree murder. Once juveniles are in criminal court, they are treated as adults, but the tension with the substantive goals of the juvenile legal system remains (Singer, 1996). Juvenile justice principles emphasize the best interests of the child, rooted in rehabilitative ideals which conflicts with the criminal court rationality of deterrence, incapacitation, and retribution. Though similar due process requirements apply to juveniles in criminal court, including the legal standard to determine competence to stand trial or to negotiate a plea, these protections can conflict with the need to establish that juveniles are different from adults in terms of their maturity and understanding of legal consequences (Tobey et al., 2000; Viljoen & Wilgrove, 2008). The use of prior convictions to sentence juveniles more harshly, to justify their waiver to criminal court or to enhance their adult sentences makes providing competent legal representation more imperative (Feld, 2003, 2017).

During a criminal trial, attorneys must prove that their clients are not beyond redemption (Trounstine, 2016). Attorneys act as advocates for youths and must comprehend the elements of juvenile justice that make it different from a criminal justice process (Kempf-Leonard, 2010). They are also responsible for augmenting a youth's understanding of the trial (Tobey et al., 2000). They are expected to be well versed with the knowledge of adolescence, youth development, and family histories; being familiar with appropriate defense strategies and coordinating with other agencies that juvenile clients may have been involved with (Jones, 2004).

The demand and need for legal services for juveniles became more commonplace as the number of juveniles arriving in criminal court increased. The criminalization of delinquent behaviors in the 1980s was propelled by an extraordinary amount of attention from media on crimes committed by impoverished youths (Bishop & Feld, 2014). Though such crimes were rare occurrences, the political response during this time was to be tough on crime (Benekos & Merlo, 2008; Bishop & Feld, 2014; Hagan, 2010; Simon, 2007; Singer, 1996). Several states changed the process of transfer, creating a combination of judicial waiver hearings, automatic exclusions and/ or direct filing by prosecutors (Bishop & Feld, 2014; Butts & Travis, 2002; Fagan & Zimring, 2000; Mulvey & Schubert, 2012). Prosecutorial discretion expanded in the early 1990s, with more direct filing of cases in criminal court instead of juvenile court (Griffin et al., 2011). States also lowered the age jurisdiction of juvenile court, sending more adolescents directly to criminal court (Allard & Young, 2002).

The number of juveniles in criminal court also increased due to statutory exclusion laws. Twenty-nine states passed statutory exclusion laws that allowed the criminal court's exclusive jurisdiction over specified offenses committed by juveniles (Rovner, 2016). Statutory exclusion provisions categorize juveniles by the charges filed, and the charges filed determine which court has jurisdiction over the case (Zimring, 2010). Importantly, once held criminally responsible, juveniles are subject to adult sanctions, including receiving life sentences (Seeds, 2018). Other amendments included applying mandatory LWOP sentences for juveniles convicted in criminal court (Kokkalera & Singer, 2019). Notably, there is no consideration of age or life circumstances in mandatory penalties (Nellis, 2012). Thus, the ability to relate a defendant's adolescence to a judge or jury at the time of sentencing became irrelevant if the offense carried a mandatory penalty of LWOP.

## The Right to Counsel in Parole

Generally, due process protections for post-conviction, fact-finding hearings are limited. For instance, a convicted individual is not entitled to a hearing when being transferred between prison facilities (*Meachum v. Fano*, 1976). Parole boards are viewed as an extension of the state prison complex. In some states, the department of corrections includes an office of parole. Other states have a separate, independent state parole agency that works in conjunction with the department of corrections. Importantly, the expansion of due process rights to prison administration proceedings is restricted to avoid abrogating the executive agency's discretion in maintaining order (Adams, 1994).

To maintain its administrative structure and inquisitorial nature, state parole boards have resisted formalization of due process rights to those seeking parole. But given the highly discretionary nature of parole decision-making, scholars have advocated for due process rights in the parole process, including the right to counsel (Moriearty, 2017; Russell, 2014), raising the burden of proof, and the right to a written decision from the parole board (Russell, 2014). Parole hearings may be characterized as trials where juvenile lifers are expected to present a case for their release, and hence the assistance of legal counsel becomes crucial (Kokkalera, 2021; Kokkalera & Singer, 2019; Russell, 2014; Trahos, 2016). Furthermore, parole decisions are increasingly based on detailed guidelines and actuarial instruments that assess reoffending risk, requiring due process protections (Thomas & Reingold, 2017).

State parole boards with discretionary release procedures typically hold three types of hearings. A parole candidate appears for their initial or first hearing after serving a minimum amount of time, as adjudicated at the time of sentencing, or determined by the state's correctional agency. Following the initial hearing, the parole board as a unit decides to grant or deny parole. If denied parole, then the parole candidate can appear for a review hearing after a period of time, ranging anywhere between one and 15 years (Kokkalera & Singer, 2019). Once granted parole, either at the initial or subsequent hearing, an individual on parole must comply with conditions that can apply to all aspects of life. If any stipulated terms are violated, the individual may be returned to custody and face a parole revocation hearing, where the parole board decides to either suspend their parole or release them back to the community.

A series of Supreme Court decisions have attempted to clarify if the right to counsel exists in parole proceedings. In *Morrissey v. Brewer* (1972), two individuals in Iowa challenged their parole revocations. Parole was revoked based on their parole officers' written reports, and they were immediately returned to the custody of the nearest state prison, without a formal hearing. Morrissey and his co-petitioner challenged their revocations on the ground that their due process was denied because they were not allowed to counter the parole officer reports. The Supreme Court, agreeing with Morrissey, held that, an individual's liberty when under community supervision

> includes many of the core values of unqualified liberty and its termination inflicts a "grievous loss" on the parolee and often on others. It is hardly useful any longer to try to deal with this problem in terms of whether the parolee's liberty is a "right" or a "privilege". By whatever name, the liberty is valuable and must be seen as within the protection of the Fourteenth Amendment. Its termination calls for some orderly process, however informal.
>
> (1972, p. 482)

The Supreme Court's interpretation of an orderly process included a right to written notice of the violations, an opportunity to present evidence, the right to confront opposing witnesses, the parole board's authority to decide the issue and a written report of the hearing but refrained from determining the right to attorney representation (*Morrissey*, 1972, p. 489).

The *Morrissey* decision left it to states to determine if the right to counsel applied to parole revocation hearings. A year after *Morrissey*, the Supreme Court was confronted with the question of whether an individual was entitled to a hearing if probation was revoked. The decision in *Gagnon v. Scarpelli* (1973) drew parallels to parole, because the revocation of probation too resulted in a loss of liberty. While supporting the need for some due process protections for probation revocation, including an informal hearing, the Supreme Court did not fully support the right to counsel. Instead, it held that to avoid turning any revocation hearing into an adversarial proceeding, a case-by-case approach is necessary to determine if an individual required the assistance of counsel. An individual can request the relevant authority for an attorney to assist with their case, but it is up to the parole board to determine if counsel is needed and if not, reasons must be presented.

Following *Morrissey* (1972) and *Gagnon* (1973), some states clarified that the right to counsel extended only to parole revocation hearings. Seventeen states currently provide legal representation at parole revocation hearings which includes states with mandatory parole, but four states allow attorney presence where the costs are borne by the individual whose parole is revoked (Kokkalera & Singer, 2019). Again, the extent of the right to legal assistance may vary. For instance, in California, the right to counsel applies to all revocation hearings, where the individual can request for an attorney at a preliminary or final revocation hearing (Zucker, 2005). A similar right is available in the state examined, where an appointed counsel's services are paid for by the state. If a request is not made, then the individual on parole forfeits the right to counsel.

Whether the right to counsel applies to other parole hearings is less straightforward. In *Greenholtz v. Inmates of Nebraska Penal Complex* (1979), the Supreme Court was confronted with the issue of whether procedural due process requirements apply to initial parole hearings. The case arose out of Nebraska where the Board of Parole conducted two types of hearings: initial parole review hearings and final parole hearings. Initial review hearings were held for every incarcerated individual regardless of parole eligibility, where the Board examined their institutional record and conducted an informal interview with the inmate. Following this initial interview, the Board could grant a final hearing or deny release with stated reasons and schedule a subsequent initial hearing within one year. If the Board scheduled a final hearing, then it notified the individual of the day and time, and the hearing allowed them to present evidence, call witnesses, and be represented, though the state did not provide an attorney if an individual could not afford one. Following the recorded hearing, the Board could decide to grant or deny parole and provide a written decision.

Incarcerated persons in Nebraska prisons brought a class action suit against the Department of Corrections arguing that their denials were unconstitutional because the Board's procedures denied them due process. The District Court after trial concluded that the procedures of the Board did not satisfy due process requirements and that the incarcerated individuals had a similar "conditional liberty" interest as noted by the Supreme Court in *Morrissey* (1972). On appeal, the Court of Appeals for the Eighth Circuit, also agreed with the District Court. However, the Supreme Court reversed the decision of the Eighth Circuit.

According to the Supreme Court, a state's parole statute that provides for the "possibility" of parole does not trigger a reasonable presumption of due process protections. Unlike parole revocation, where there is some loss of liberty, an initial parole hearing merely offers hope of release, and not its presumption. As a result, it is up to states to determine the mechanisms by which parole release should be determined. For the Supreme Court, Nebraska's parole statute provided a valid opportunity to be heard and present evidence and did not compromise the ability to present suitability for release. With regard to right to counsel, the Supreme Court ruled that Nebraska's procedure to allow incarcerated individuals to appoint counsel of their choice was constitutionally sufficient and as such, mandatory state-appointed counsel was not necessary.

*Morrisey* (1972) generally guaranteed the right to a hearing, noting that it did not cost more than incarcerating individuals for multiple years, but did not specify that due process requirements included the right to counsel. As such, states can continue to bar counsel presence during the parole hearing since there is no absolute requirement to provide legal representation (Annitto, 2014; Russell, 2016). The high costs of providing counsel in addition is a deterrent for states (DBH, 1980). In a review of parole procedures across all 50 states and the District of Columbia, Kokkalera and Singer (2019) found that 16 state parole boards do not allow any type of legal representation and 17 states appoint counsel for parolees facing revocation proceedings, presumably to comply with the Supreme Court's decision in *Morrisey* (1972).

Instead, states have relied on the *Greenholtz* decision (1979) to avoid creating guidelines that create a "protectible expectation" of parole—one that can be enforced through appellate review (Thomas & Reingold, 2017). No other case has shifted this stance, meaning that it remains a state's prerogative to legislate if parole candidates have the right to counsel (Annitto, 2014; Bierschbach, 2012). Some states have moved forward by introducing guidelines that warrant the need for legal representation, though such representation is typically accessible only if a parole candidate can afford it.

The latest interpretation of the right to counsel in parole hearings comes in the context of juvenile lifers previously sentenced to automatic LWOP terms and now eligible for parole hearings. As noted, two decisions of the highest appellate court in the state examined clarified that a meaningful opportunity for juvenile lifers (whether they received LWOP or life with parole) includes the right to legal representation at the initial parole board hearing. Specifically, the decision guaranteeing legal representation to those who received automatic LWOP terms noted that "the parole process takes on a constitutional dimension that does not exist for other offenders whose sentences include parole eligibility".[5] Both decisions requiring legal representation noted that since juvenile lifer candidates lack the knowledge and resources necessary to contest statements of those opposing their release, the assistance of counsel would enable them to prepare for and demonstrate their readiness for community supervision. The appellate court characterized legal representation as integral in parole hearings that "involves complex and multifaceted issues that require the potential marshalling, presentation, and rebuttal of information derived from many sources".[6] The state legislature subsequently amended its criminal code, requiring the appointment of counsel for juvenile lifers in the parole process. The court decisions and subsequent codification of the right to counsel provides an opportunity to understand how access to legal assistance enables a meaningful opportunity for release for juvenile lifers.

## Notes

1  The Sixth Amendment: "In all criminal prosecutions, the accused shall enjoy the right to a speedy and public trial, by an impartial jury of the State and district wherein the crime shall have been committed, which district shall have been previously ascertained by law, and to be informed of the nature and cause of the accusation; to be confronted with the witnesses against him; to have compulsory process for obtaining witnesses in his favor, and to have the Assistance of Counsel for his defense".

2  *Prerogative Regis* is a royal prerogative formed by one of the central tenets of common law, which gives the King the sovereign power to rule over subjects (see Blackstone W. Commentaries in Curtis, 1976)

3  Legal Scholar Roscoe Pound famously described the juvenile court as "a tribunal more awesome in its abuse of power than the Star Chamber" (Pound, 1937 cited in Feld, 2017).

4  The Supreme Court did not rule on the right to a transcript, and correspondingly the right to an appellate review but encouraged states to consider providing these rights.

5  Decision available upon request.

6  Decision available upon request.

# 3 What about Effective Legal Representation for Juvenile Lifers?

## Defining Attorney Effectiveness

The definition of attorney effectiveness was first provided by the Supreme Court in *Strickland v. Washington* (1984) as conduct by the State or conduct by counsel that is so prejudicial that it undermines the functioning and results of the trial. The challenge of ineffective assistance can only be made on appeal, where the burden of proof is incredibly high because the appellant must show that their legal assistance fell below an "objective standard of reasonableness" (Primus, 2007).[1]

However, the *Strickland* (1984) decision was not clear on the standards to determine effectiveness of counsel. In three death penalty cases in the early 2000s, the Supreme Court clarified that the American Bar Association (ABA) Standards are useful guides in what constitutes effective legal assistance.[2] Specifically, the Supreme Court in *Wiggins v. Smith* (2003) found that ABA Guideline 11.8.6 (1989) can be viewed as a standard of determining effectiveness of counsel, where an attorney must do all that is possible to provide evidence of mitigation in reducing the sentence applicable to a case. According to the guideline, an attorney is expected to investigate and report on several aspects of their client's life including their medical history, educational history, military service, employment history, family and social history, prior adult or juvenile correctional experience, rehabilitative potential, and any other expert testimony concerning these factors. On an appeal against a death sentence, an individual can argue that their trial attorney's investigation on mitigating factors was less than adequate in relation to the ABA guideline's requirements. In the majority opinion by Justice Sandra Day O'Connor, the ABA guideline was characterized as a "well-defined norm", where an attorney's departure from the guideline would constitute ineffectiveness (*Wiggins*, 2003, p. 524). Previously, in *Williams v. Taylor* (2000) and later in *Rompilla v. Beard* (2005), the Supreme Court also referred to ABA Standards as rules that might reasonably explain effective

DOI: 10.4324/9781003196914-4

assistance. In sum, the right to counsel has little meaning if attorneys do not comply with certain performance standards (Mlyenic, 2008).

Whether the effectiveness of counsel standard applies in other legal settings is still open to interpretation. For instance, a claim of ineffective assistance of counsel has been raised in cases involving the termination of parental rights with mixed success (Calkins, 2004). Similarly, the ineffectiveness standard has been applied to immigration proceedings. In 1989, the Board of Immigration Appeals, the appellate forum of the immigration court system, held that that ineffective assistance of counsel may violate due process rights in removal proceedings of noncitizens (*Matter of Lozada*, 1989).[3] In *Padilla v. Kentucky* (2010), the Supreme Court clarified that criminal defense attorneys must advise noncitizen clients about deportation risks of a guilty plea, and failing to do so would constitute ineffective assistance of counsel.

Whether juvenile defendants can raise ineffective assistance claims has received some scholarly attention. Fedders (2010) argues that those who are concerned with the implementation of the right to counsel in juvenile court per *In Re Gault* (1967), should be equally concerned with a lack of avenue for juveniles to bring ineffective assistance claims in appellate review. The lack of appeals may be due to a combination of unfamiliarity that juvenile clients can bring up an ineffective assistance claim and a reluctance on the part of appellate courts to entertain the issue. Consequently, juveniles can bring up ineffective assistance claims to rectify the problem of deficient representation in four ways:

> (1) establish a standard of professional conduct, albeit a floor of what is constitutionally permissible conduct rather than a ceiling of zealous advocacy; (2) deter actionable misconduct through the setting of these norms; (3) perform a signaling function for attorneys that delinquency practice is a serious one; and (4) identify those lawyers who have practiced ineffectively and who should therefore be considered for removal from the panel of court-appointed lawyers.
>
> (Fedders, 2010, p. 819)

When there is a statutory provision for the appointment of counsel, then the right becomes meaningful only when the right to counsel is effective (Calkins, 2004). Generally, attorneys representing youth clients are expected to provide their assistance with a combination of advocacy, competence and counseling (Tobey et al., 2000).

### *Effectiveness and Type of Attorney*

Broadly, attorneys in criminal and juvenile courts can be distinguished as public defenders, appointed attorneys, and private or retained attorneys

(Feeney & Jackson, 1991). Public defenders are attorneys whose organizational structure is like state prosecutors and their resources are tied to what the state can provide. Appointed attorneys offer private legal services but are appointed by the court to represent an indigent defendant if they have volunteered to do so. In the state examined, appointed attorneys are certified in the areas they practice in and comply with state public defender agency performance standards. Retained attorneys are paid either directly by a client or may represent them *pro bono*.

Prior research on the type of attorney effect has been mixed across different criminal legal settings. According to Iyengar (2007), representation by public defenders was related to shorter federal sentence lengths by 16%, relative to cases with retained attorney representation. Likewise, Anderson and Heaton's study of Philadelphia attorneys (2012) found that having a public defender was related to a lower conviction rate by 19% and lower odds of a receiving a life sentence compared to representation by an appointed counsel. However, Williams (2013) noted the opposite effect in a study using data from the four largest Florida counties where a defendant with a public defender was less likely to have their charges dismissed, more likely to be detained pre-trial and more likely to be convicted, relative to a defendant with a retained attorney. Contrary to these findings, Hartley et al. (2010) found no direct effect of type of counsel on any process outcome in criminal court including release, reducing charges, incarceration, and sentence length. Similarly, Williams (2002) tested whether type of attorney was associated with criminal court outcome, and found that having a retained attorney, relative to an appointed attorney was not associated with the likelihood of receiving probation, an incarceration term, or even sentence length.

In juvenile court, Guevara et al. (2008) found that youth represented by a retained attorney had a higher likelihood of out-of-home placements (i.e., detention) and lower likelihood of dismissal of charges. Carrington and Moyer's (1990) study revealed that youths with retained attorneys were less likely to be adjudicated and more likely to have the charges dismissed. In contrast, public defenders and state appointed counsel in juvenile court seem to fare worse. For instance, Armstrong and Kim (2011) discovered that public defenders increased the odds of out-of-home placements for youths in Missouri while Clarke and Koch (1980) observed that youths represented by court-appointed counsel were somewhat more likely to be committed than those with private counsel. However, location of the juvenile court may matter, as noted by Peck and Baudry-Cyr (2016) who find that the presence of counsel is a mitigating factor for a sample of Northeast youths but not Midwest youths. The variation in the influence of attorney type of juvenile court outcomes could be related to how legal representation is provided to minors (Kokkalera et al., 2021).

Public defenders have received a significant amount of attention, especially in the context of juvenile defendants. One explanation offered as to why public defenders fare worse in terms of ultimate outcomes is their heavy caseloads which can impact their representation to the detriment of their clients (Drinan, 2017). Juvenile defense work is perceived to be of low status with high turnover rates and little training (Bishop & Fraizer, 1991; Drinan, 2017). Other research has found that juveniles did not view public defenders as adversaries, but that retained attorneys were perceived as more effective and likely to spend more time preparing for the case (Erickson, 1974).

One obvious gap in the research is the limited understanding of how type of attorney is associated with outcomes for juveniles in the criminal legal system. Zane and colleagues' (2020) study examined the effect of type of legal representation for juveniles in criminal court across 40 large urban counties. They found that public defenders fared better in terms of decreased odds of conviction, lower likelihood of incarceration and lesser sentence lengths, relative to youth defendants with retained attorneys. However, a significant limitation is that the dataset was from proceedings concluded in 1998 and the variation in access to legal representation is different today (see Kokkalera et al., 2021). Still, an important implication of Zane and colleagues' study is that states should put their resources behind state public defender agencies. As noted by Anderson and Heaton (2012) in their study of attorney representation for adult criminal defendants, disparities created by the incentive structures for appointed attorneys do not provide an adequate opportunity to prepare for cases as thoroughly as public defenders.

There is some research on the role of legal representation in the parole process. Bell's study (2019) of 426 youth offender parole hearings in California found that candidates with retained attorneys were more likely to be granted parole. Appointed attorneys do not seem to fare as well because of the incentive structure in California since legal fees are capped at $400 (Bell, 2019; Caldwell, 2016). In Michigan, researchers found that appointed attorneys are at the forefront of providing holistic legal assistance by balancing "(a) the information that system actors rely upon to make resentencing and parole decisions, and (b) the resources that paroled juvenile lifers need to survive upon release" (Husseman & Siegel, 2020, p. 902). In sum, the function of type of attorney representation seems to be contingent on time and place. More comparative research is needed to fully uncover how legal representation enables a meaningful opportunity of release for juvenile lifer candidates.

Drawing on data from the state examined in this book, Kokkalera (2021) found that there is no "attorney effect" in terms of release, but type of attorney was associated with the length of an interval term. A parole candidate must wait anywhere between one and five years for another hearing following a denial of parole in the state examined. Such interval terms provide parole boards with additional discretion that determines the ultimate amount of time a candidate will serve in prison (Friedman & Robinson, 2014; Kokkalera, 2021). For juvenile lifer parole candidates, having an appointed attorney (through the state public defender agency) is related to lower odds of a maximum interval term of five years whereas having a retained attorney is associated with an increased likelihood of a maximum interval term (Kokkalera, 2021). An important takeaway is that attorneys can influence the amount of time that a candidate will ultimately serve in prison. Still, as the findings in this book will illustrate, there is more to unpack in terms of *how* legal assistance is provided throughout the parole process including during the hearing (*own emphasis*).

## Attorney Effectiveness in Parole

Parole candidates are coached in a variety of strategies to present themselves as suitable parolees by in-prison case managers, the incarcerated, and legal counsel (Martel, 2010). A successful parole candidate can employ a strategic presentation of a particular identity—that of an individual who is capable of being a law-abiding citizen if released. During the hearing, a parole candidate attempts some form of "impression management" by constructing plausible accounts of their crimes, relating their rehabilitative efforts, and presenting appropriate release plans (Radelet & Roberts, 1983). Goffman (1957, 1968) viewed impression management as the selective disclosure of oneself through social cues and communication. In parole hearings, attempts to establish a credible presentation of self through appropriate emotional expressions, words, and behaviors are contested by parole board members and opposers of parole (Lavin-Loucks & Levan, 2015). Parole boards hold more power than those seeking release, especially since the latter has been convicted of a crime and possess as Goffman (1968) termed, a "spoiled identity" (Lavin-Loucks & Levan, 2018).

As Martel (2010, p. 428) describes, parole decision-making is "negotiated partly by playing the parole game, that is actively managing the parole board's impressions, and participating in the (re)construction of one's identity as a parolee". The criminal legal system advantages those who have the capacity to present themselves in a credible manner (Rossmanith, 2013). The presentation of self is tied closely to how parole candidates competently relate all that is required including an explanation for the crime, their efforts at rehabilitation, and evidence of community support if released. The lack of competency can be an artefact of age, developmental issues, mental health diagnoses, and/or inability to access appropriate assistance. In

Michael's case, for example, his record in prison can be viewed as above average with few disciplinary issues and regular participation in institutional programming. Yet, his inability to relate his suitability for community supervision hinders the possibility of release.

To represent juvenile lifer candidates like Michael, an effective attorney should be "attuned to the Board's expectations" and will "coach or advice the client to conform to them" (Aviram, 2020, p. 29). Unlike in a criminal trial or adjudication hearing in juvenile court where an attorney does almost all the talking before a judge and/or jury, attorneys are less vocal in a parole hearing. While an attorney need not actually present their knowledge during the hearing, they must be familiar with their client's family history, background, and other situational factors at time of offense (Fedders, 2010). An attorney is further expected to enhance a parole candidate's presentation of self. Though a parole hearing is not nearly as adversarial as a criminal trial, some questions can be accusatory in nature and observations made at the hearing can transform the meaning of a candidate's words (Lavin-Loucks & Levan, 2015). It is up to an attorney to prepare their candidate to avoid engaging in any narrative that appears to excuse their criminal conduct.

How candidates present themselves may further depend on whether their attorneys take the lead in the parole hearing. At the trial stage, an attorney facilitates effective legal assistance by complying with what the client wants. Even in juvenile delinquency proceedings, an attorney is expected to provide guidance that is consistent with a child's best interest but must also be cognizant of the child's expressed interests (NJDC, 2019). In a parole hearing, juvenile lifer candidates must explain their crimes to the parole board which occurred many years ago and under a myriad of circumstances. An attorney's role involves preparing a juvenile lifer to engage in difficult conversations with the parole board and to adequately highlight their adolescence at the time of the offense. One way is for the attorney to make an opening statement that succinctly summarizes their client's plea for release. Alternatively, an attorney can prepare the juvenile lifer candidate to make a powerful opening statement because parole boards may not be receptive to attorneys who speak on behalf of their candidates. The extent to which an attorney facilitates juvenile lifer parole candidate's presentation further depends on the amount of assistance provided. The nature of legal representation for parole hearings varies considerably from trial work, where the preparation is focused almost entirely on preparing the parole candidate client for the hearing (Aviram, 2020).

Attorneys are also expected to prepare a juvenile lifer to respond to the parole board and other actors present in the parole hearing. Apart from the juvenile lifer parole candidate and attorney, parole board members can hear testimony from a district attorney or police department representative on behalf of the victim or the victim themselves. Supporters of parole can also submit written statements and testimony. Parole board members create their own impressions of the parole candidate and may seek information during the hearing to further corroborate their views (Cohen, 2014; Hawkins, 1983, 1986). Members have the power to freely question the parole candidate and interrupt if responses are unsatisfactory (Medwed, 2008).

### Attorney Effectiveness for Juvenile Lifer Candidates

Post-*Miller*, parole boards are expected to evaluate a juvenile lifer's parole eligibility with an explicit consideration of their reduced culpability at time of offense and potential for rehabilitation (Russell, 2014, 2016). In facilitating a meaningful opportunity, an attorney should enhance a juvenile lifer's presentation of self, by drawing on their biography to mitigate culpability and relate their rehabilitative efforts.

Attorneys can draw on the general and specific references to a juvenile lifer's adolescence at time of offense. The general reference to adolescence is found in neurological evidence and relied on by the courts as an explanation for a juvenile lifer's reduced criminal responsibility (Grisso, 2017; Levick & Schwartz, 2013; *Roper v. Simmons, 2005*; Scott & Steinberg, 2008; Scott et al., 2015). On average, ongoing brain development in adolescents precludes them from making well-thought decisions and increases their proclivity for being impulsive and indulging in risky behaviors (Steinberg, 2014). Justice Kagan in her majority opinion for *Miller* (2012) noted that decision-makers must be attuned to both the generalized features of adolescence and attendant circumstances leading up to the crime (Marshall, 2019). Many juvenile lifers have experienced difficult childhoods, often victimized by violence, abuse, and neglect, struggled with other experiences like inadequate housing and learning disabilities (Caldwell, 2012; Drinan, 2017; Feld, 2017; Nellis, 2012). Several may have been victimized by others in their larger community, for instance, being forced to join criminal gangs for protection (Singer, 2017). Attorneys are expected to draw on these adolescence-related factors by conducting a close review of a juvenile lifer's biography. Deeply personal questions from the parole board are directed at a juvenile lifer, about their childhood, family life, and community (Cohen, 2014). Attorneys are expected to prepare their juvenile lifer clients to answer any question that comes their way—no matter how personal.

In conjunction with presenting their mitigated culpability, a juvenile lifer candidate must show that they have outgrown violent behavior and no longer pose a threat to the community (Bell, 2019). Attorneys must be equipped to present their clients in the best light before the parole board. There is no specific checklist for parole board members to use in determining if an incarcerated individual is rehabilitated (Palacios, 1994). For attorneys, this means that they must not only deal with the lack of specific criteria for release, but they must be able to advise their incarcerated clients to present their rehabilitative efforts in the best way possible (Trahos, 2016). Ideally, attorneys should be able to recognize failures of the correctional system in providing rehabilitative avenues and make the case that their clients have not failed. Though providing juvenile lifers a meaningful opportunity implies that states should provide lifers with sufficient chances to rehabilitate themselves (Drinan, 2012), lifers are often the lowest priority for any programming. Even when programs are available, they can be random or inadequate and the access to such programs can be curtailed due to several reasons including budget cuts and criticisms of programs in the press (Trounstine, 2016).

For those whose parole is revoked, attorneys have the additional responsibility of highlighting the issues that juvenile lifers face in reentry. Juvenile lifers who are released, return to their communities that may have contributed to their crimes (Mears & Travis, 2004). They are expected to enroll in after-care programs that may not be individualized to their needs, especially in terms of dealing with the consequences of their institutionalization at a much younger age (Mulvey & Schubert, 2012). Thus, during revocation review hearings, juvenile lifers and their attorneys face the complicated task of defending their actions during their time on parole supervision, apart from making the case for their re-release.

For any parole hearing, an attorney's preparation of a juvenile lifer involves challenging a pre-determined perspective of the crime. A juvenile lifer's blameworthiness is reflected in the more horrific elements in the commitment offense. Juvenile lifers are already deemed criminally responsible for lethal acts of violence in earlier stages of the criminal legal process (Bishop & Feld, 2014; Feld, 2017). The facts of the offense are found in the juvenile lifer's case file and discussed again during the hearing before the parole board. As a result, parole decision-making may be based on a more dispositional point of view—one that is focused on "dangerousness" rather than on understanding the situational circumstances of the crime (Binder & Notterman, 2017). Moreover, the Supreme Court's decisions in *Graham* (2010) and *Miller* (2012) did not address the paradox of considering the adolescence of a juvenile lifer who is now a middle-aged adult (Boone, 2015). While advocating for their client's mitigated culpability at time of offense, attorneys are confronted by the parole board's deference to the facts of the offense found at trial (Gonzales, 2015). Previous research on parole decision-making has found that statutory factors including seriousness of the commitment offense and number of felony convictions are strong indicators of parole votes (Carroll & Burke, 1990; Kinnevy & Caplan, 2008; Morgan & Smith, 2005).

In other words, considerations of a juvenile lifer's reduced culpability and rehabilitation are challenged by current discretionary release practices that are rooted in the principle of risk avoidance and blameworthiness (Drinan, 2017; Feld, 2017; Tonry, 2019) Drawing solely on the facts of the offense to deny parole can be inconsistent with the Eighth Amendment (Russell, 2016). Still, parole boards expect candidates to explain their role in the offense and for their account to match with trial records (Medwed, 2008). Jurisprudential reasoning of the reduced culpability of juvenile lifers suggests how a juvenile lifer might resist taking responsibility for the crime (Cohen, 2014). But parole boards may not buy into their diminished culpability if candidates do not accept full responsibility for the crime. Attorneys must therefore balance the presentation of reduced culpability without excusing their juvenile lifer client's responsibility for the crime.

## Notes

1   Several factors can affect the effectiveness of counsel including prosecutorial misconduct (*Miller v. Pate,* 386 U.S. 1 [1967]; *Napue v. Illinois,* 360 U.S. 264 [1959]; *Mooney v. Hollohan,* 294 U.S. 103 [1935]); *Berger v. United States,* 295 U.S. 78 [1935]); failure to disclose any exculpatory evidence to the defense (*U.S. v. Bagley,* 437 U.S. 667 [1985]); *Brady v. Maryland,* 373, U.S. 83 [1963]); failure to present a plea deal (*Missouri v. Frye,* 132 S.Ct. 1399 [2012]), and potential conflicts of interest for the attorney (*Wood v. Georgia,* 450 U.S. 261 [1981]; *Holloway v. Arkansas,* 435 U.S. 475 [1978]).
2   The American Bar Association is a voluntary organization for legal professionals. For more information see: www.americanbar.org/about_the_aba.html
3   Though there is variability in state and federal case law where some courts have ruled that there is no due process right to counsel in removal proceedings (MacLeod-Ball & Werlin, 2016), there is some support to adopt the *Strickland* standard of ineffective assistance of counsel for noncitizen criminal defendants (McDermid, 2001).

# 4 Study Setting, Data, and Methods

## Study Location

The Supreme Court's decisions put the onus on states to establish when and how juveniles sentenced to LWOP would become eligible for early release. States opted to provide resentencing hearings or parole board hearings, or some combination of the two (Drinan, 2017; Kokkalera & Singer, 2019). The state examined in this book is among a handful to respond to the *Miller* decision (2012) by providing immediate parole eligibility if those sentenced to LWOP have served a minimum term of their life sentence. First, immediately after *Miller* (2012), the highest appellate court in the state ruled that any LWOP sentence, i.e., a mandatory or discretionary one, is unconstitutional even when applied to juveniles convicted of first-degree homicide. The decision also made the *Miller* (2012) decision retroactive and directed the parole board to allow juvenile lifers previously serving LWOP to appear for a hearing if they have served a minimum of 15 years (like their counterparts sentenced to life with parole). Consequently, juvenile LWOP parole hearings began the following year. Next, the state legislature amended the criminal code to replace LWOP for first-degree murder with life with the possibility of parole after 20 to 30 years for individuals who were below the age of 18 at the time of the offense.

However, juvenile lifer candidates who received parole-eligible life sentences and other long-term maximums have been appearing before the state parole board for decades. In 2015, the highest appellate court in the state ruled that a meaningful opportunity of release for all juvenile lifers (whether they received LWOP or life with the possibility of parole) includes the right to legal representation at their parole board hearing. At this time, the right to an attorney is presumed to apply to only initial hearing which is the first parole eligibility hearing after serving the stipulated minimum term. However, juvenile lifers can seek representation for review or revocation review hearings, though there are no guarantees of appointment unlike at the first

DOI: 10.4324/9781003196914-5

hearing.[1] Since the 2015 ruling, the state public defender agency appoints an attorney for a juvenile lifer candidate one year before they become eligible for a parole hearing.

The state parole board comprises seven members who are each appointed for a term of five years by the Governor. Members are expected to represent different fields including law enforcement, prosecutor offices, legal defense, psychology, sociology, and social work. Once appointed to the parole board, members are expected to serve full time and cannot hold any other salaried public office.

Parole decisions are made based on a review of the candidate's case file and a formal hearing. A case file includes all the relevant information about the commitment offense including arrest reports, trial documents, criminal history before and after imprisonment, and institutional record of programming. Parole board members also review letters in support of or against the candidate's release. Candidates are expected to submit a parole plan, outlining their proposed housing situation, medical care, employment opportunities and community support. Case files can run into hundreds of pages, and all parole board members are expected to become familiar with the case file before the hearing.

A formal hearing is held once the individual is eligible for parole. The date is scheduled after discussion with their attorney and then requested with the parole board staff. A formal parole board hearing is viewed as critical to determining if a candidate is truly deserving of parole (Bell, 2019; Cohen, 2014; Dawson, 1966; Hawkins, 1983; Martel, 2010). For all those with parole eligible life sentences, the hearing takes place in the Board's central office. The candidate makes an opening statement, appealing for their release and their attorney may make a similar statement as well. Next, members take turns to question the candidate, ranging from the facts of the commitment offense to institutional adjustment, rehabilitative efforts, and particulars of the parole plan. Following questioning, supporters of parole can make a statement. Then, a member from the victim's family or victim advocate or any other members opposing release can present statements of objection, or in some rare instances, support for release. The district attorney's office where the commitment offense occurred is required to submit a statement and may send a representative to testify during the hearing. At the end of the hearing, the candidate and/or their attorney can make a closing statement, reiterating the plea for release.

Following the hearing, parole board members meet to vote on the candidate's release and a detailed written decision is produced. The legal standard for determining release is repeated in every decision statement—that parole is granted so long as the individual will not violate any laws and that their release is compatible with public safety concerns. A two-thirds majority is required for a grant of parole, i.e., at least five out of seven members. Written decisions are expected to stipulate reasons for grant or denial, and in granting decisions, terms and conditions of parole must be mentioned.

## Data Sources

Prior research on examining the role of legal representation in deliberative processes has shown that interviews can reveal how attorneys view their role in assisting clients (Maier, 2009). An attorney for the purpose of this study is defined as anyone who has represented at least one juvenile lifer candidate before the parole board. Attorneys are typically employed in (1) the state public defender agency; (2) private practice and appointed by the public defender agency to represent a juvenile lifer; (3) private practice where they are hired directly by the juvenile lifer candidate to represent them; or serve as (4) student attorneys from legal aid clinics in law schools.

A list of attorneys was created when compiling a dataset of written decisions produced by the parole board (between 2005 and 2018), by contacting a legal aid clinic at a law school and by reaching out to the state public defender agency. The list produced 55 attorneys who have appeared before the parole board at least once on behalf of a juvenile lifer. Five attorneys were excluded from interviews, did not participate or were otherwise ineligible to be interviewed.[2] Another three attorneys' latest contact information was not updated online and were therefore not reachable. For 47 attorneys, information was gathered through a website search. Attorneys were contacted first through LinkedIn (if available), or by e-mail, and followed-up via phone. Two attorneys were contacted directly by phone. Thirty attorneys responded stating interest, following which ten interviews were conducted between September 2018 and June 2019.

Of the ten interviewed, seven are male and three are female. Attorneys varied by their type of employment: one attorney was employed with the public defender agency at the time of representation; six attorneys were engaged in private criminal defense practice but served as appointed attorneys in the parole process; one was a private attorney who was retained through the juvenile lifer client, and two appeared before the parole board as student attorneys but have since joined a defender agency and prosecutor's office. At the time of the interviews, professional experience ranged from 1 year to 40 years.

Additionally, the distribution of the sample matches the overall variation of attorney type across 207 juvenile lifer parole board hearings between 2005 and 2018. Based on data collected from written decisions, attorneys were present in 110 hearings. Of those 110 hearings, 18 (16.36%) had student attorneys, 14 (12.72%) had private attorneys retained by the candidate,

13 (11.82%) had public defenders, and 65 (59.09%) hearings had attorneys who were appointed by the public defender agency to represent candidates.

The interview involved a list of semi-structured, open-ended interview questions and was recorded with the permission of the attorney. Semi-structured interviews allowed for attorneys to bring up new concepts or topics that were not covered in the questions (see also Naughton et al., 2015; Seale, 2012; Weingraf, 2001). On average, an interview took around 35 minutes, and the longest interview was nearly 1 hour. Notes were also taken when the interview was being conducted to verify responses or ask follow-up questions during or after the interview. Notes were not coded for analysis but were helpful in creating themes and writing the findings.

The author also had access to 101 parole board hearing audio or video recordings that took place between 2005 to 2013. These 101 hearings involved 65 juvenile lifer parole candidates. Of these hearings, 20 included the presence of an attorney. Unlike at a criminal or civil trial, attorneys are not the lead players in the parole hearing. At most, attorneys read prepared statements at the beginning or at the end of the hearing on behalf of their juvenile lifer candidates. The author further transcribed portions of the hearing where attorneys made any statements (opening or closing). The number of interjections made by attorneys during these hearings were then counted, specifically when attorneys interrupted a parole board member to clarify a line of questioning or to question a parole board member's stance on a particular aspect of a case. Interestingly, since the hearings occurred prior to the *Miller* decision, representation at the hearings was primarily through student attorneys because right to counsel was not guaranteed until 2015.

## Analytical Methodology

All interviews were transcribed and read line-by-line. The transcribed interviews were uploaded into NVivo Pro 12, a data analytical software. NVivo Pro 12 allows for an in-depth analysis of texts and is suitable for producing a deeper understanding of the topic of inquiry. While multiple qualitative methods may be appropriate for this type of data, discourse analytical techniques were employed (see Starks & Trinidad, 2007 as one example).

Discourse analysis techniques have been particularly useful in producing rich data from relatively small datasets (Talbot & Quayle, 2010). Discourse analytical techniques allow for an exploration of "socio-cultural discourses and scientific knowledge" (Naughton et al., 2015, p. 353). Put more simply, discourse analytical techniques draw on language and texts as sites where social meanings are produced (Tonkiss, 2012; Willig, 2008). For instance, Naughton and colleagues (2015) employ discourse analytical techniques to evaluate how juvenile court judges interpret the principle of the "best interest of the child" in custody cases in Ireland. Examining the words used by judges allowed the authors to go beyond the content and identify beliefs that motivate their understanding of the best interest principle.

Prior research has not been able to identify a formal, standard approach to discourse analysis (Tonkiss, 2012; Wells, 2011), though generally coding techniques identify words, phrases, and sentences that display a participant's understanding of a topic. The coding emphasizes how individuals produce discourse about an issue, keeping in mind that they are products of the discourse themselves (Edley, 2001). Like other qualitative methodologies, discourse analysis is an interpretive process that relies on a close review of the organization and details of the examined words, phrases, and sentences.

The goal of discourse analysis techniques, unlike content or conversational analysis, does not necessarily involve accounting for every single line of the text under review. Instead, the coding reflects key themes or arguments, makes associations between those themes, and pays attention to how the themes are characterized by those relating them (Tonkiss, 2012). The ways of speaking about a topic and how the topic is understood are viewed as interpretive repertoires (Potter & Wetherell, 1987). Interpretive repertoires can be viewed as shared meanings or shared framing of a certain topic or issue. The coding is organized around these interpretive repertoires, i.e., codes are created first to draw patterns between them. The coding follows the process of abduction in assembling or discovering data. Abduction constitutes one of the first steps of any interpretative process where facts are sorted to achieve an understanding of the issue at hand, and as a result, tentative hypotheses are made (Åsvoll, 2013). Once the abductive steps produce a tentative hypothesis, then deductive explanations can be sought after.

All interviews were read three times before beginning the coding cycle. In the first round, codes were derived from interview questions. For example, segments were coded "preparing for trial" and "preparing for parole" based on a direct question. Similarly, "type of attorney" was coded from responses from attorneys about their current professional position. In the next round, original codes were created. These codes were applied to smaller segments of the transcribed interviews, single sentences and sometimes phrases unlike in the first round of coding. Examples of original codes include "preparing materials", "time spent on preparation", "preparing lifer for testimony", "reviewing case files", "reviewing *Miller* factors", "expected outcome", and "parole board impression". These constitute interpretive repertoires following an abductive process of identifying larger themes.

Once all the interviews were coded, the third round of the coding cycle involved organizing the codes into a hierarchical coding structure (Creswell, 2013; Miles et al., 2014). There is some debate on what might constitute a satisfactory threshold in coding themes (Campbell et al., 2013). In this study, a code was categorized as a sub-theme if it emerged across at least five attorney interviews, establishing it as a threshold, i.e., 50% of interviews should be attached to a code for it to be deemed significant. A parent code was created after reviewing each subtheme, and a parent code was recognized as a theme only if it emerged in all ten interviews.

For the 20 parole board recordings, a quantitative coding scheme was created to track: (1) if attorneys made an opening and/or closing statement during the hearing; and (2) the number of interruptions where an attorney interrupted a parole board member's questioning or response to the candidate. The results from the quantitative coding scheme were useful in relating to how the discourse analytical themes played out in the parole board hearings.

## Notes

1  A review hearing can take place after one to five years following a denial of parole. Revocation review hearings determine if a candidate's parole should be revoked, returning them to incarceration, or if they should remain under community supervision.
2  One attorney's contact information was unavailable, one attorney refused participation, two attorneys worked in the same office as an attorney who was interviewed and declined participation to avoid conflict of interest in responses, and one attorney was recently nominated for a judgeship and could not participate.

# 5 Contextualizing the Role of Counsel in Parole

## Protecting Rights

All interviewed attorneys qualified their role as necessary to protect the due process rights of their juvenile lifer client. An attorney who has his own private practice but serves as an appointed attorney for parole candidates succinctly summarized how his presence allows for the protection of legal rights:

> I'm there to protect my client, so that they are treated fairly throughout the process. I have access to records and whatnot, and have the correct information presented before the parole board. So, like I said, that every procedure is followed, that all applicable laws are followed.

An attorney's presence before and during the hearing is viewed as integral to ensuring that procedural and substantive legal rights are not violated in a highly discretionary setting. Other professionals such as psychologists may be called to testify but they may not be familiar with legal issues that can arise in a parole hearing, making the presence of an attorney more imperative (Kempf-Leonard, 2010).

All interviewed attorneys mentioned that their presence during the parole hearing is necessary as a due process protection, even for a parole candidate who is familiar with the process. As related by another attorney about a client who has appeared multiple times before the parole board:

> I just had this hearing and this guy had been before the parole board on a number of occasions. And not so much for the presentation, although the presentation to the parole board . . . they just said you know . . . I think the opening line from the Chairman, was like "isn't this easier?" You know, basically, this is the person we'd like to talk to. This person. Not the person from the last hearing. It was a recognition that this

DOI: 10.4324/9781003196914-6

person had somehow transformed their approach to parole and that's not something that he would have done on his own. And so, that's good. It's not about me. It's still about him, but he wouldn't have been able to do that by himself.

Attorneys are trained to communicate with authorities who have discretionary powers, and as a result, they are in a position to direct a compelling narrative. The hearing is still about the candidate, but legal assistance allowed the client to be more prepared for the type of questions raised by the parole board. Attorneys can recognize the shortcomings of a juvenile lifer client's previous performances at hearings and appropriately strategize as to how to enable a client to present themselves more effectively in a proceeding.

Attorneys are bound by the statutory and administrative rules of professional conduct to protect the rights of their juvenile lifer clients (Mlyenic, 2008). An attorney who has worked as a criminal defense lawyer for nearly forty years described his assistance in the parole process as "client-centric":

I don't believe that the lawyer should be doing anything but assisting and keeping the record . . . basically, making sure that the record is complete and making sure that the record reflects everything that the client is trying to say. It's quite focused.

The emphasis is on maintaining a complete record and training juvenile lifer clients to relate all the appropriate facts during the hearing. Other attorneys also expressed a similar professional responsibility of making sure that it's a "parolee-run ship", and that an attorney will interject during a parole hearing only when needed like when there is a serious misconstruction of fact or the law.

As evidenced from the quantitative content analysis of parole hearings, Table 5.1 (below) shows that most attorneys presented opening and/or closing statements. An interruption was coded when an attorney interjected during a dialogue between a parole board member and candidate to provide a comment or clarification. As seen below, some attorneys did not interject at all during the hearing.

Attorneys often opt to provide an opening or closing statement to provide a summary of the juvenile lifer candidate's case. In Don's hearing, his student attorney summarizes the case for release:

[Don] completed various educational and training courses. He has an extensive prior work history and he completed various treatment programs. Throughout his whole history, every single evaluation of [Don] has said positive things about his character and work ethic. This is the

*Table 5.1* Coding Scheme for Parole Hearings with Attorneys (2005–2013)

| Parole Board Hearing | Type of Attorney | Did Attorney Make Opening Statement? | Did Attorney Make Closing Statement? | Number of Interruptions |
|---|---|---|---|---|
| Barry (2008) | Student | Yes | Yes | 1 |
| Charles (2010) | Student | Yes | Yes | 2 |
| Chris (2008) | Student | Yes | Yes | 0 |
| Chris (2013) | Appointed | Yes | Yes | 7 |
| Clarence (2011) | Student | Yes | Yes | 2 |
| David (2006) | Student | Yes | Yes | 0 |
| David (2011) | Student | Yes | Yes | 0 |
| Don (2007) | Student | Yes | Yes | 2 |
| Hector (2012) | Student | Yes | Yes | 1 |
| Jose (2011) | Student | Yes | Yes | 1 |
| Keith (2006) | Student | Yes | Yes | 0 |
| Miguel L (2011) | Student | Yes | Yes | 0 |
| Miguel V (2013) | Student | Yes | Yes | 2 |
| Ralph G (2010) | Student | Yes | Yes | 0 |
| Ralph G (2013) | Student | Yes | Yes | 0 |
| Ralph H (2009) | Retained | No | Yes | 4 |
| Robin (2012) | Student | Yes | Yes | 2 |
| Rod (2012) | Retained | Yes | Yes | 2 |
| Tim (2010) | Retained | Yes | Yes | 4 |
| Tony (2011) | Retained | Yes | Yes | 9 |

most relevant and the most important evidence that this board should focus on, in deciding whether or not [Don] is fit for parole. [Don]'s institutional records and accomplishments provides the most certainty that one's release can be compatible with the welfare of society. [Don] is 47. He is no longer an irresponsible and reckless teenager. His release does not pose a threat to society.

Though the hearing took place prior to the *Miller* (2012) decision, the attorney makes a point to raise Don's adolescence as a factor for consideration in terms of his lesser culpability ("irresponsible and reckless teenager") and rehabilitative capacity ("institutional records and accomplishments").

Furthermore, attorneys describe their advocacy as social work, therapy, and emotional support. An attorney who has represented over ten juvenile lifers at multiple parole hearings compared advocacy during the parole process to a spotter during weightlifting:

So, right, the person lifts the weight, and you try not to touch it because you hope that they could do it by themselves, but you don't know, or like a swimming lesson for little kids. You don't want them, but you got to have the person there. So, um . . . you can't . . . have a rule to not have a person but I always say, you know, there will certainly be a time where I get to the point with somebody where I say, "you don't need me . . . not only do you not need me, but you're certainly going to do better without me, that this is going to look better for you to just get up there and do your thing and not have a lawyer sitting next to you . . . because who needs that?" . . . And I think most of the time, you don't need that. But you can't not have it as an option. That would be really, really bad!

Though the parole board wants to hear almost exclusively from the parole candidate, as simply put by this attorney, not having legal representation "would be really, really bad" even for a juvenile lifer who is socially and emotionally equipped for a hearing. An attorney's role at the hearing is compared to that of a spotter in weightlifting, where a spotter steps up only when the athlete is unable to complete the task at hand. At a parole hearing, all the heavy lifting in terms of relating readiness for parole supervision is on the juvenile lifer candidate. The candidate is expected to be prepared to narrate the best version of themselves and present a compelling account of why they would be successful on parole. An attorney is not expected to interrupt or interject, or even expect any questions from the parole board. However, when a candidate is unable to respond appropriately, or may not know the correct response, then an attorney can step in and assist their client.

## Preparing for Parole

Preparation for a parole hearing was described as immense, time-consuming, and involving tremendous coordination with state and local agencies. Several attorneys related that the hours spent on reviewing and preparing for a parole hearing can exceed the time spent on other matters. Some were able to provide specific timelines, but generally, the time needed to review multiple records varies by type of case and available resources. For instance, student attorneys had only three months to prepare for the hearing which did not include the time taken to secure the appropriate records from prison facilities, medical or mental health service agencies, schools, and social service departments. These records which can run into hundreds of pages were collected by the supervising attorney in advance and then distributed to the student attorneys to review. Student attorneys worked on a case as part of their academic training during a single semester, meaning all their working hours were spent on preparing for a single parole hearing. For attorneys who have multiple clients, months can go into just preparing for the parole case since their work is distributed over time. One attorney mentioned that he worked on a juvenile lifer parole case for nearly 18 months, but other attorneys who were appointed to represent a juvenile lifer stated that on average, they spent at least six months reviewing their case files and then a few weeks writing the memo for the parole board. An additional challenge as noted by another attorney is that some records may be lost or difficult to read, especially for those who were incarcerated decades earlier.

Several attorneys voiced difficulties in coordinating between agencies such as the candidate's prison facilities and the parole board staff. An attorney, who has represented the same juvenile lifer at multiple hearings, explained:

> There is an institutional file that has all of the disciplinary records, mental health records, activities, and everything—that's crucial. The parole board . . . I would say is . . . unhelpful generally, although some of the staff there are very nice, and they do what they can. But the policies are such that they make it as difficult as possible. But you can get in there to see what's there . . . by appointment, and that's a good thing to do soon.

The process of reviewing documents, through appointment and with permission of the parole board can slow down an attorney's preparation for the parole hearing. As noted by this attorney who deals with multiple agencies for his client, the issue is not with those working with the parole board, but to work with multiple agencies at the same time. It often takes more than one visit to do a complete review of the file from each agency including the parole board.

Preparation also implies being ready even beyond all the necessary paperwork prior to the hearing. One student attorney who has appeared for the same juvenile lifer parole candidate for an initial and subsequent review hearing related the importance of being completely prepared for anything:

> If someone doesn't have preparation or isn't ready for what they're going to hear . . . .. I mean just that example of just one hearing . . . where the DA came and misconstrued one line in the record and that's just stuck in that file forever.

As noted, during the hearing, attorneys can inform the parole board about any discrepancy in the file submitted on behalf of their client. Such preparation, therefore, enables attorneys to interject when there may be some misconstruction of fact, or to clarify any misrepresentation. In Chris' hearing for example, his attorney interrupts a line of questioning to clarify his client's specific request for parole:

> Attorney K: I would just like to clarify a little about this specific request that we're making for parole because the request to be paroled to the from and after is conditioned on the completion of the [Sex Offender Treatment Program]. It is my understanding that a positive vote from the board would allow him to go, would encourage the DOC to transfer him to the [Facility]. He would have to complete [the Sex Offender Treatment Program] to be deemed by the [Facility] to have completed the program and at that point, the positive parole vote would kick in and he would go to his, from an after.

Several attorneys further related that a significant aspect of preparing for parole involves coaching the juvenile lifer client for testimony such as practicing appropriate responses to anticipated questions. An attorney who was appointed to represent multiple juvenile lifers explained:

> Most of my work is going in there and obviously me knowing everything so that they can be properly advised but at the end of the day, it's really about preparing them so they can talk about everything that they're supposed to talk about in a hearing. They can distill everything that they need to, and they can answer all the questions that have been asked and they can do it the right way. There are just so many things that they can be questioned about, and any of it can become grounds for a parole board member to say, "oh what's going on here is something to be concerned about" . . . and you have to prepare for all of them and you have to have a good answer for them. I mean they need to be prepared to give a good answer in a smart way. They need to be prepared for it and need to answer it.

Attorneys are expected to anticipate any question that could conceivably be posed during the parole hearing. The review of the case files becomes crucial, and attorneys review previous hearings to see what questions may come up again if those questions were perceived as not having been answered satisfactorily. One attorney also noted that he coaches his juvenile lifer clients to not minimize any aspect of their criminal conduct during the hearing. Another similarly remarked that for a client with an erratic history of adjustment, the best response is to accept the record and avoid excuses that appear to minimize their conduct.

All attorneys specifically pointed to the *Miller* (2012) decision as a framework to draw on in writing the memo making the case for release. One attorney who has represented juvenile lifers pre-and post-*Miller* notes that attorneys should relate factors presented in the Supreme Court decision:

> We would look at all the factors that *Miller* would say we need to look at. Are they . . . well, number one—What caused the crime? Number two, what steps have they taken? And leading up to, showing that they are able to return to society without putting out any risk to others. So, their risk assessment scores, psychological assessment, there's many steps that are taken for juvenile lifers.

*Miller* factors can be drawn on refer to two main concepts. First, adolescent reasons for offending that precipitated the commitment offense and second, the rehabilitative efforts undertaken by the juvenile lifer to prepare for community supervision. The constellation of factors that can be presented is drawn from multiple assessments over decades of incarceration.

Most attorneys reported that their role in the parole process is held to a different standard post-*Miller*. A review of a juvenile lifer's case is meaningful when their adolescence is recognized as a context for the offense. In other words, reasons for the crime may be general such as being impulsive, or specific such as childhood traumas, parental neglect and abuse, poverty, the influence of older delinquent peers, or joining a neighborhood gang (Singer, 2017). Adolescence-related reasons for an offense can be highlighted in the memo submitted to the parole board as well as during opening and closing statements at the hearing. For example, one attorney explained that she drew on the notion of historical trauma in explaining the mitigated culpability of her juvenile lifer client:

> I've learnt through the course of this case, a whole lot about historical trauma. And it gave me a whole different appreciation about getting to know more than I traditionally had about a person, their background and family. . . . You know I've spent then a lot of time thinking about my client's background, even their birth . . . how their neonatal care was. But not really back to, hey what happened to your mom when she was 20. So, this gave me a huge appreciation for how important that can be, which I've carried with me, since I did it.

Going deep into a client's background and context for the offense provides an attorney with a greater understanding of reasons that enable violence. Historical trauma, therefore, serves as a compelling reason to mitigate culpability. Other specific reasons to mitigate culpability that attorneys have been able to draw on include drug use, familial abuse, emotional difficulties, psychological factors, and official diagnoses such as learning disabilities.

Several attorneys stated that they prefer to present documented evidence of rehabilitation to support their client's release on parole. One attorney who has 40-plus years of criminal defense experience makes the case for an individual's desistance from criminal behaviors as good evidence for success on parole:

> And his . . . N******* for example, um . . . when he first got in, he was getting a lot of disciplinary tickets. And then, you can see on a timeline, as he got older, those went way down and once the *Miller* decision came out, it was zero. He was really behaving.

Most of those who were incarcerated as juveniles have poor initial institutional adjustment, usually the result of having to act tough and establish their identity in prison (Levick & Schwartz, 2013). Moving into a prison as an adolescent and then spending more than a decade in prison means that a considerable period of institutional time comes under scrutiny. Attorneys can highlight change in behavior over time, emphasizing when the violation of institutional rules ceased and the type of programs that their juvenile lifer client participated in up until their parole board hearing.

## Managing Expectations

Most attorneys reported that they would schedule a parole hearing only after their clients expressed that they were prepared for the hearing. Still, the possibility of parole may be more realistic for only a few candidates. For instance, one student attorney stated:

> This is what we have to do as attorneys, and what we do every day in court, is that we have to manage expectations. If that's what the client wants to say, that's their right but we need to let them know that you can't expect that to be their most successful route. . . . It would be difficult to . . . you'd be looking at this with your client, and not so much in a "what do we need to do to get you parole?" but it would be more as if "ok, what do we need to do to make this case more realistic?" for you.

The ultimate expectation of being released on parole is influenced by the juvenile lifer's case history and their testimony at the hearing. For juvenile lifers with an erratic institutional history, the strategy is to explain whether the possibility of parole is a real possibility. More crucially, it is up to the attorney to ensure that their client is aware that the outcome may not be what they expect—despite jurisprudential reasoning on their side.

The expectation of release is moderated by how well a juvenile lifer can do at the hearing. Several attorneys noted that the public nature of a parole hearing is challenging for juvenile lifers. The anxiety of appearing in a public setting to discuss one of the worst moments of their lives is a daunting task for even the most prepared juvenile lifer. Not only are they expected to answer questions candidly, but they must do so in the presence of victim's families, and sometimes the media. As explained by an attorney who was employed as a public defender at the time of the parole hearing:

> The other thing that was bothersome to me about the whole parole hearing process is that it really focuses on verbal skills. And we had so many clients with language processing problems, that it seems so unfair that they could be doing so wonderfully but they are just unable to articulate what's going on . . . or have a misstep in their language, or understanding of a question that then puts them in a position that they shouldn't be in. And so, there should be, I mean I don't really have a concrete idea, but there should be some other way for folks that have those sorts of issues, to still have a similar chance.

Juvenile lifers are expected to share intimate details of their lives, and some are much less prepared than others to appear in a public setting where their words are recorded and shared with others. Another attorney, who served as an appointed attorney for three juvenile lifers, stated that one of her clients was "so anxious, he said if he can't do it this time, he doesn't know if he could do it again". A juvenile lifer has the right to delay or decline an appearance before the parole board even if a date of eligibility has been made. In such instances, a juvenile lifer may expect to never be released on parole and it is up to their attorney to determine if it is worth changing their client's mind.

While juvenile lifers willing to appear for a parole board hearing are usually hopeful of release, most attorneys expressed that managing their optimism of being granted parole can be difficult. Importantly, the possibility for release is closely related to the ability to take full responsibility for the offense. An attorney who has practiced for over 40 years and represented two juvenile lifers spoke about one of his cases to highlight the importance of taking responsibility for the crime before the parole board:

> One kid went in and killed the clerk. N****** was the lookout in the parking lot, and he could not understand how he could be guilty of a murder if he didn't pull the trigger. No matter how often you explained it, he wouldn't get it. I went to his family . . . they're all sitting around

and saying, "how could he be convicted, he didn't pull the trigger". They just don't get the concept of joint venture.

A juvenile lifer candidate may find it difficult to accept full responsibility for their commitment offense, especially when they did not pull the trigger. They buy into the legal argument that they are not as blameworthy as their codefendants but may not know how to convince others (Cohen, 2014). While this example relates to a juvenile lifer's limited role in the shooting, other juvenile lifers may have little recall because the crime was committed in a less than conscious state or due to the influence of alcohol and drugs (Marquez-Lewis et al., 2013). Attorneys are placed in a particularly precarious position in managing the expectations of release for those who are unable or unwilling to accept responsibility for the offense. There is not much that can be done beyond explaining the legal implications of maintaining full or partial innocence before the parole board.

Attorneys manage their clients' expectations for release by developing and maintaining a personal relationship. The attorney-juvenile lifer client relationship is described as intimate, built on trust, and of mutual respect. One major aspect of maintaining the relationship is the extent to which attorneys communicate with their juvenile lifer clients. One student attorney provided an example of the relationship developed with his client:

> He didn't call me every day to discuss a factual issue with this case, but he called me every day because I was his advocate and he liked having an advocate looking out for him. And I think it emboldened him in a positive way that you know, somebody was fighting for me. That I think . . . I mean not to say that that is the only benefit for representation for a lifer hearing but that certainly is one of the benefits . . . it's that . . . you know, for our parolee in particular, he was 16 when he committed the crime, he was incarcerated for 15 to 20 years, and he did not have a lot of people who were advocating on his behalf. I think it took him a little bit of time to warm up to us and open up to the idea that we were genuinely just there to do the best that we could for him. That really got him excited about the idea of getting out of prison.

For some juvenile lifers, attorneys may be the only source of social and emotional support. Attorneys are counted on to communicate regularly, and communication can go beyond discussions of their parole case. Consistent conversations with an attorney can serve a purpose beyond securing a positive parole vote for juvenile lifers. For some attorneys, those relationships can develop into a friendship, sustained over the years and even after their client is out on parole. As described by an attorney who has represented the same juvenile lifer client at multiple hearings, "we are friends, of some kind. I personally care about him a lot".

Managing a juvenile lifer's expectation of release is closely associated with their attorney's expectations from the process. The obvious answer is that attorneys expect their clients to be granted parole. But six attorneys stated that a shorter interval period which is a lesser amount of time following a denial is a positive outcome. As related by an attorney who has practiced for nearly 40 years and represented multiple juvenile lifers before the parole board:

> I mean I may be misreading, but when the parole board gives you a five-year [interval term], you're in bad shape but if you get a three-year [interval term], maybe the parole board thinks that there is hope for you and you don't need five years to straighten things out. Three years would be enough time.

A shorter interval term than the legally stipulated maximum of five years gives a juvenile lifer hope of eventual release. It suggests that more time is not needed or more work is not necessary than what is already being done to prepare for parole. One attorney stated he would recommend a shorter interval term after consulting with his clients in their memo and during the hearing especially if release appeared to be a remote possibility at the time.

## Challenging Practices

All attorneys expressed that the parole hearing was a difficult setting—a vulnerable experience for their clients, unpredictable, and formal without applying any strict rules of evidence. Two distinct challenges were described in relating how parole hearings are conducted. First, attorneys were concerned about the amount of discretion afforded to parole board members in the type of questions that they are allowed to ask. One female attorney who has been appointed to represent multiple juvenile lifers gave an example of a line of questioning in a parole board hearing to portray the amount of discretion:

> It wasn't anywhere in the record but apparently, in the victim impact statement, the brother had said that the victim had just come from a sickle cell anemia benefit. She says, "do you know where the victim had just come from?", and he says, "no," and she says, "a sickle cell anemia benefit!", and then she's just looking at him, and he says, "oh, I didn't know that". She goes, "Oh! You didn't know that?". . . . I mean, what's that got to do with anything? I just thought it was so unfair, and

I didn't know whether it was an MO, where you dig up a fact that's buried somewhere and when the person doesn't acknowledge it or recognize it, pretend that you think they're hiding something.

While there is some predictability to questioning, there can be questions that neither the candidate nor attorney can anticipate due to the wide latitude in administrative guidelines. In the scenario described by the attorney, the question was entirely unexpected. But parole board members can ask any question that relates to the parole candidate's record. Minimizing any aspect of the record can be perceived as hiding relevant information or appearing to not accept full responsibility for the crime. Depending on the line of questioning, both the parole candidate and their attorney can perceive unfairness in a parole hearing.

Second, the discretionary powers of the parole board produce a lack of predictability in the parole hearing, not just in terms of the questions asked but the extent to which responses are relied upon to justify a decision. For instance, a student attorney who has appeared twice on behalf of the same juvenile lifer client remarked:

> You really can't know how um . . . it's going to go until you're in that hearing. Then when you leave, you have no idea what it's going to be . . . or what it was that informed their decision. . . . Which I think is actually the biggest problem . . . with representing people at parole hearings, in general and in particular, juvenile lifers. That there is no level of predictability to that, and there should be.

Parole board members are attuned to any fact that may emerge from the hearing. Parole board members can maintain a neutral stance during the hearing, as explained by the student attorney, but following the hearing, members meet to discuss their impressions of the parole candidate and can draw on any aspect of the hearing to justify their decision. Even though the parole board is expected to reflect on the *Miller* factors, as another attorney who has represented multiple juvenile lifers noted, "they're not as specific in their decisions as people would like them to be". For attorneys, there is no routine checklist either in terms of the questions or in terms of the criteria that need to be considered in presenting a decision granting or denying parole.

Some attorneys were more forthcoming about their concerns of how the parole board operates. An attorney explained that the structure of a parole hearing reflects the parole board's general outlook on releasing a segment of individuals:

> So, if it turns out that you happen to have all the people with a similar mindset, so then it means you don't have questions thrown in that

would allow . . . say more of a spotlight on somebody's childhood, or something like that, if you end up with all folks who think adolescent brain development is not all that important, let's say for example. So then, you have a different kind of hearing than when you have people there who are asking those kinds of questions that you're talking about.

For attorneys, the composition of the parole board can determine the type of questions that are likely to be raised. If most parole board members operate with a retributive mindset, then lines of enquiry will reflect those beliefs. Other attorneys suggested that more members with backgrounds in clinical psychology, education, social work, and legal defense should be appointed to the parole board to enable a hearing with more questions about a juvenile lifer's mitigated culpability and how their adolescence impacted their adjustment to prison.

While the parole board's line of questioning in recent years has been shaped by *Miller* (2012), some questions are driven by political and media pressures. A few attorneys specifically pointed to an incident several years ago that shifted the general attitude of the parole board. In 2010, a parolee shot and killed a police officer, and most parole board members resigned soon after. The aftermath of that incident seems to have lingered ever since. An attorney who has practiced for nearly 40 years and represented multiple juvenile lifers pre-and post-*Miller* observed:

> And I haven't seen the statistics in a while. I wish that may be more people would get paroled more regularly. And yes, I know there was this huge thing that happened back in 2010 that sort of sent everything spinning for many, many years . . . and so, I sometimes wish more liberal leaning people would be put on the board. But, you know, you sort of have to take what you can get.

Another attorney described this as a systemic belief that parole should not be granted as a matter of routine. Similarly, a student attorney stated that he was not expecting his client to be paroled because "nobody had been paroled in that time". Attorneys are challenged by the perception that parole board members are operating with the presumption to deny, unless proven otherwise. For juvenile lifer candidates, their commitment offense is a serious crime that cannot be overlooked by the parole board. Those who face opposition from the victim's family, prosecutor, or even the media are further disadvantaged by the parole board's pressure to avoid making any decisions that may look bad. Therefore, politics at the time can also matter and it is up to attorneys to strategize on how to overcome the political nature of parole decision-making in presenting an effective case for their client's release.

# 6    Conclusion—In Defense of Juvenile Sentenced to Life

In establishing the right to legal representation for juveniles, the Supreme Court in *Gault* (1967) noted that a youth cannot be expected to conduct the duties associated with putting up an effective defense without an attorney (Fedders, 2010). Juvenile defense attorneys are expected to become familiar with a juvenile client's biography, specialized laws, and recent research on adolescent development (Cooper et al., 1998). In addition to traditional legal obligations in an attorney-client relationship, attorneys representing youths are expected to function as advocates and social workers (Kempf-Leonard, 2010; Tobey et al., 2000). To that end, juvenile defense advocacy extends beyond case parameters (Ortega, 2015).

Effective legal advocacy is essential in "highly discretionary contexts that are outcome-determinative" (Simkins & Cohen, 2015, p. 352), like parole board hearings. Jurisprudential reasoning and subsequent changes in the law requiring the appointment of counsel suggests that legal representation enables the meaningful opportunity of release. Empirical studies are often quick to assess the influence of legal representation by accounting for the presence of counsel. But focusing on attorney presence alone to explain outcomes can miss key variables that are either irreducible to quantitative indicators or not contained in outcome data sources (Lynch, 2017). As findings from the qualitative analysis reveal, whether a juvenile lifer is released on parole is not the only way to gauge an attorney's role in enabling a meaningful opportunity. Attorneys provide an important due process protection by facilitating a fair hearing that does not proceed on any erroneous information (Arbour, 1973). The influence of attorney presence may be further related to how an attorney is appointed, who they represent and the resources available to present a good defense.

## Due Process and Zealous Advocacy

For attorneys representing juvenile lifers, advocacy not only includes presence at the hearing, but more importantly preparation for the parole board

DOI: 10.4324/9781003196914-7

hearing. Multiple records over decades are reviewed to concisely present a juvenile lifer client's plea for release. The amount of time spent on a case and volume of preparation may vary by type of attorney due to differential access to resources. A significant aspect of the preparation involves training the juvenile lifer candidate for testimony and to respond to all anticipated questions from the parole board. Such preparation enables a juvenile lifer candidate to credibly present their willingness to be successful on parole.

All attorneys emphasized that their preparation includes effectively relating the mitigated culpability of their juvenile lifer clients and their evidence of reform as contemplated in the *Miller* (2012) decision. A candidate can be trained to not only draw on generalized features of adolescence like impulsivity, susceptibility to external influences and transiency but also their personal biographies to lessen criminal culpability. In preparing for a parole hearing, attorneys can similarly assist juvenile lifers to use the defense of their youth.

A meaningful opportunity for review as imagined by the Supreme Court also involves recognizing "demonstrated maturity and rehabilitation" (*Graham*, 2010). In the context of parole, maturity may be evaluated by a candidate's institutional behavior (Bernhardt et al., 2010). To that end, several attorneys mentioned that they rely on documented chronological evidence to show proof of reform. Poor initial adjustment can be explained as the result of having to act tough on arriving in prison (Levick & Schwartz, 2013). Lack of consistent participation in programs can be explained by budget cuts restricting rehabilitative options in prison, and limited access to those sentenced to life (Drinan, 2017; Lynch, 2016; Trounstine, 2016).

Juvenile lifers may expect a positive vote of parole based on jurisprudential reasoning that they are less culpable due to their adolescence at time of offense. Several attorneys repeatedly stated that they present their client's reduced culpability but at the same time, encourage clients to accept responsibility for the crime to increase the possibility of parole. Attorneys expect a line of questioning regarding the parole candidate's version of the crime. Any diversion from the reported facts can be perceived as minimizing responsibility. Though adolescent status at time of offense explains why a juvenile lifer might resists taking full responsibility for the crime in a parole board hearing (Cohen, 2014), parole boards continue to expect all candidates to account for their role in the offense (Lavin-Loucks & Levan, 2015; Martel, 2010; Medwed, 2008).

Parole board members rely on the case file to get the candidate to acknowledge their role in the commitment offense. Questions about certain aspects of the crime that may not be true or cannot be recalled can be perceived as unfair by both the attorney and their client. It is perceived as especially unfair if the inability to recall is later used to deny parole. The onus, therefore, is on attorneys to prepare their clients to effectively present their reasons for the offense as mitigating circumstances but not to excuse responsibility.

The expectation of release is further moderated by a juvenile lifer candidate's performance at the parole board hearing. Not all are equally equipped in presenting the reasons for their release. Some candidates can express deep remorse, recognizing the harm caused and still be denied because they are unable to accept responsibility for the crime (Martel, 2010). Others may be too anxious to relate all that is needed to convince the parole board that they are ready for community supervision (Rossmanith, 2013). Michael, as noted, has not been able to present a credible narrative of why he deserves to be released on parole, despite documentation that shows a low risk to reoffend. A juvenile lifer's preparedness for the hearing may be further impacted by their relationship with their attorney. A trusting relationship goes a long way in giving a juvenile lifer the confidence to appear before the parole board.

Effectiveness of legal assistance can further be captured in a juvenile lifer's presentation of self which involves a credible narration of remorse, responsibility, and redemption (Singer & Kokkalera, forthcoming). Attorneys are trained and equipped to assist juvenile lifers in presenting a compelling defense of their character, one that highlights life stories of victimization, neglect, and abuse (Caldwell, 2012). To enhance their client's presentation of self, attorneys must balance their adversarial tactics with the requirements of an administrative hearing that expects to hear almost exclusively from the parole candidate. State appellate courts and/or legislatures that buy into the need for legal representation for juvenile lifers should create specialized standards for professional conduct and training (Fedders, 2010; Mlyenic, 2008).

An interesting finding is that attorneys do not view a grant of parole as the only positive outcome that reflects a meaningful review of their client's case. Depending on the case and after multiple conversations with their juvenile lifer client, several attorneys stated that they suggest asking for a shorter interval between hearings instead of a grant of parole. The parole board can grant a maximum interval term of five years following a denial, and as such a shorter interval suggests that lesser time is needed for the candidate to be ready for parole. As one attorney noted, a shorter interval suggests that "there is hope" of eventual release. Receiving a shorter interval term may be viewed as another way that attorneys facilitate a meaningful opportunity.

## Creating Meaningful Policies for a Meaningful Opportunity

Discretionary release practices of parole boards are geared toward parole candidates who have committed crimes as adults. Parole guidelines are largely suggestive or advisory and it is up to members to choose which listed factor is most salient in deciding release (Ball, 2011; Thomas & Reingold, 2017). Some members may be operating with a retributive mindset with an expectation of an imagined amount of time that must be served irrespective of how qualified a candidate may be for release. Without clear directives, parole release can be seen as arbitrary and capricious if candidates are not certain of having the guidelines applied equitably (Ball, 2011; Nuffield, 1982). For instance, Bell's study (2019) finds that release decisions are largely arbitrary and capricious because the candidate's race affected decision outcomes, regardless of other variables. Attorneys are acutely aware of the discretionary nature of parole decision-making. Even though attorneys influence shorter interval terms for parole candidates (Kokkalera, 2021), there are no standards for explaining the interval term given by the parole board (Haas & Magrath, 2016). For both juvenile lifer candidates and their attorneys, parole decisions can be vague or specific in justifying denial of parole (Drinan, 2017).

While attorneys facilitate a meaningful opportunity, denial decisions may not consider the reduced culpability or rehabilitative efforts of a juvenile lifer. In such instances, denials may be appealed but there is no guaranteed right to counsel in the appellate process. In other words, juvenile lifers who wish to challenge their decision must bear the costs of the appeal. Furthermore, courts are generally reluctant to review parole decisions and the standard of review is high. The Supreme Court's decision in *Greenholtz* (1979) clarified that a minimal standard of due process would apply only when a state's parole statute creates an expectation of release. States have since been careful in crafting guidelines that do not create an expectation of parole that might become enforceable (Thomas & Reingold, 2017). To that end, challenging a parole denial is an appeal that is often avoided, and as a result, the right to appeal is less impactful without the right to counsel.

While the right to legal representation is a substantive right for juvenile lifers, many adult lifers lack access to counsel services. An overwhelming number of those incarcerated today are over the age of 60, many of whom are serving lengthy indeterminate terms or life sentences. Some states have a geriatric release program (see Dujardin, 2017) but their release decisions suffer from the same issues as parole hearings for juvenile lifers (Drinan, 2017). Therefore, discretionary release practices could impact other segments of the incarcerated populations, and thus, legal representation may be beneficial for all parole candidates.

While the data in this book represents the parole process in one state, other states are making similar legislative changes (e.g., California, see Bell, 2019, Caldwell, 2016). Still, this study provides the groundwork for research in states that allow for legal representation in parole hearings for juvenile lifers, and for states considering extending the right to counsel in the parole process. While the interviewee sample is relatively small, the use of discourse analytical techniques allowed for a deeper exploration of the topic (see Talbot & Quayle, 2010). Other dimensions of attorney representation enabling a meaningful review could have been missed since juvenile lifers and parole board members were not surveyed. The pool of recordings is also small and took place prior to *Miller* (2012). Yet, the hearings provided a glimpse of how attorneys operate during the actual hearing and reiterate the point that much of the legal assistance occurs prior to the candidate's appearance in front of the parole board.

## A Call to Recognize the Defense of Youth

The findings from this study raise empirical questions that are worth pursuing in the future. For instance, what are parole board member impressions of legal representation? Do juvenile lifers support attorney presence at parole hearings? Investigating these perspectives will paint a fuller picture of how attorneys are enhancing a juvenile lifer's presentation of self, and in turn enabling a meaningful opportunity for release. Likewise, the role of Forensic Mental Health workers can be crucial in explaining *Miller* factors to resentencing courts and parole boards (Scott et al., 2015). Therefore, non-legal representation may be equally helpful in facilitating a juvenile lifer's possibility of release. Some states have opted for providing resentencing instead of parole board reviews, warranting an exploration of how resentencing courts draw on the reduced culpability of juvenile lifers to justify early release. More generally, there is a need to study how *Miller* (2012) and *Montgomery* (2016) have impacted the discretionary release practices of state parole boards for juveniles incarcerated in state prisons with lengthy indeterminate sentences of less than life.

The developmental status of juvenile lifers suggests that not all are equally capable of advocating for themselves and should be afforded counsel in parole proceedings (Simkins & Cohen, 2015). Michael represents one of many thousands of juvenile lifers who face the possibility of parole. Yet many, like Michael, do not have access to legal assistance in a hearing that requires a defense of their character. The right to counsel is imperative for juvenile lifers who do not have the capacity to present an effective defense of their ability to succeed on parole. The incapacity to present the best version of themselves can also apply to adult parole candidates. Legal representation in the form of presence and preparation enables a meaningful opportunity that is qualified beyond whether a candidate has secured parole. Therefore, an attorney's role in the parole process qualifies as an important due process protection, enables zealous advocacy and whose insight can push for broader institutional reforms.

# Bibliography

Adams, W. D. (1994). The prosecutorial appeal of parole: The indigent prisoner's right to counsel. *Wayne Law Review, 41*(1), 177–202.

Allard, P., & Young, M. (2002). *Prosecuting juveniles in adult court: Perspectives for policymakers and practitioners*. The Sentencing Project.

American Civil Liberties Union (ACLU). (2016). *False hope: How parole systems fail youth serving extreme sentences*. ACLU.

Anderson, J. M., & Heaton, P. (2012). How much difference does the lawyer make: The effect of defense counsel on murder outcomes. *Yale Law Journal, 122*, 154–217.

Annitto, M. (2014). Graham's gatekeeper and beyond: Juvenile sentencing and release reform in the wake of *Graham* and *Miller*. *Brooklyn Law Review, 80*, 119–172.

Arbour, P. W. (1973). The parole release decision- due process and discretion. *Louisiana Law Review, 33*, 708–717.

Armstrong, G., & Kim, B. (2011). Juvenile penalties for "lawyering up": The role of counsel and extralegal case characteristics. *Crime & Delinquency, 57*(6), 827–848.

Associated Press. (2017, July 31). 50-state examination. *Associated Press*. www.ap.org/explore/locked-up-for-life/50-states

Åsvoll, H. (2013). Abduction, deduction, and induction: Can these concepts be used for an understanding of methodological processes in interpretative case studies? *International Journal of Qualitative Studies in Educations, 27*(3), 289–307. https://doi.org/10.1080/09518398.2012.759296

Aviram, H. (2020). *Yesterday's monsters: The manson family cases and the illusion of parole*. University of California Press.

Ball, D. W. (2011). Normative elements of parole risk. *Stanford Law & Policy Review, 22*(2), 395–411.

Bell, K. (2019). A stone of hope: Legal and empirical analysis of California Juvenile Lifer parole decisions. *Harvard Civil Rights-Civil Liberties Law Review, 54*, 455–552.

Benekos, P. J., & Merlo, A. V. (2008). Juvenile justice: The legacy of punitive policy. *Youth Violence and Juvenile Justice, 6*(1), 28–46.

Bernard, T., & Kurlychek, M. (2010). *The cycle of juvenile justice* (2nd ed.). Oxford University Press.

Bernhardt, D., Mongrain, S., & Roberts, J. (2010). Rehabilitated or not: An informational theory of parole decisions. *The Journal of Law, Economics, & Organization, 28*(2), 186–210.

Bierschbach, R. (2012). Proportionality and parole. *University of Pennsylvania Law Review, 160,* 1745–1788.

Binder, G., & Notterman, B. (2017). Penal incapacitation: A situationist critique. *American Criminal Law Review, 54*(1), 1–56.

Birckhead, T. R. (2010). Culture clash: The challenge of lawyering across difference in juvenile court. *Rutgers Law Review, 62*(4), 959–991.

Bishop, D., & Feld, B. C. (2014). Juvenile justice in the get tough era. In G. Bruinsma & D. Weiburg (Eds.), *Encyclopedia of criminology and criminal justice* (pp. 2765–2773). Springer.

Bishop, D., & Fraizer, C. E. (1991). Transfer of juveniles to criminal court: A case study and analysis of prosecutorial waiver. *Notre Dame Journal of Law, Ethics and Public Policy, 5,* 281–302.

Boone, B. H. (2015). Treating adults like children: Resentencing adult juvenile lifers after *Miller v. Alabama. Minnesota Law Review, 99,* 1159–1194.

Butts, J., & Travis, J. (2002). *The rise and fall of American youth violence: 1980 to 2000.* Urban Institute.

Caldwell, B. (2012). Appealing to empathy: Counsel's obligation to present mitigating evidence for juveniles in adult court. *Maine Law Review, 64*(2), 392–423.

Caldwell, B. (2016). Creating meaningful opportunities for release: *Graham, Miller* and California's youth offender parole hearings. *N.Y.U Review of Law and Social Change, 40,* 245–304.

Calkins, S. (2004). Ineffective assistance of counsel in parental-rights termination cases: The challenge for appellate cases. *The Journal of Appellate Practice and Process, 6*(2), 179–236.

Campbell, J. L., Quincy, C., Osserman, J., & Pederson, O. K. (2013). Coding in-depth semi-structured interviews: Problems of unitization and intercoder reliability and agreement. *Sociological Methods & Research, 42*(3), 294–320.

Carrington, P. J., & Moyer, S. (1990). The effect of defence counsel on plea and outcome in juvenile court. *Canadian Journal of Criminology, 32*(3), 621–637.

Carroll, J. S., & Burke, P. (1990). Evaluation and prediction in expert parole decisions. *Criminal Justice and Behavior, 17*(3), 315–332.

Clarke, S. H., & Koch, G. G. (1980). Juvenile court: Therapy or crime control, and do lawyers make a difference? *Law & Society Review, 14*(2), 263–308.

Clear, T., & Frost, N. (2014). *The punishment imperative: The rise and failure of mass incarceration in America.* New York University Press.

Cohen, F. (1965). Function of the attorney and the commitment of the mentally ill. *Texas Law Review, 44,* 424–469.

Cohen, L. (2014). Freedom's road: Youth, parole, and the promise of *Miller v. Alabama* and *Graham v. Florida. Cardozo Law Review, 35,* 1031–1089.

Cooper, N. L., Puritz, P., & Shang, W. (1998). Fulfilling the promise of In Re Gault: Advancing the role of lawyers for children. *Wake Forest Law Review*, *33*, 651–680.

Corbin, A. M. (2015). *Role conflict among juvenile defenders in an expressed interests jurisdiction: An empirical examination* [Dissertation, Northeastern University].

Crawford-Pechukas, Z. (2019). Sentence for the damned: Using Atkins to understand the "irreparable corruption" standard for juvenile life without parole. *Washington & Lee Law Review*, *75*(4), 2147–2206.

Creswell, J. W. (2013). *Research design: Qualitative, quantitative, and mixed methods approaches*. Sage Publications Inc.

Curtis, G. B. (1976). The checkered career of parens patriae: The state as parent or tyrant. *DePaul Law Review*, *25*, 895–915.

Dawson, R. O. (1966). The decision to grant or deny parole: A study of parole criteria in law and practice. *Washington University Law Review*, *1966*(3), 243–303.

DBH. (1980). Procedural due process in parole rescission hearings. *Virginia Law Review*, *66*(4), 779–795.

Detrick, S. (1996). Inadequate legal representation of juvenile offenders in the United States. *The International Journal of Children's Rights*, *4*, 311–313.

Drinan, C. H. (2012). *Graham* on the ground. *Washington Law Review*, *87*, 51–92.

Drinan, C. H. (2017). *The war on kids: How American juvenile justice lost its way*. Oxford University Press.

Dujardin, P. (2017, April 24). Virginia questions whether to release older prisoners. *U.S. News*. www.usnews.com/news/best-states/virginia/articles/2017-04-24/virginia-questions-whether-to-release-older-prisoners

Edley, R. (2001). Analysing masculinity: Interpretative repertoires, ideological dilemmas and subject positions. In M. Wetherll, S. Taylor, & S. Yates (Eds.), *Discourse as data: A guide for analysis* (pp. 189–228). The Open University.

Erickson, P. G. (1974). The defense lawyer's role in juvenile court: An empirical investigation into judges' and social workers' points of view. *The University of Toronto Law Journal*, *24*(2), 126–148.

Fagan, J., & Zimring, F. E. (2000). *The changing borders of juvenile justice: Transfer of adolescents to the criminal court*. University of Chicago.

Faulk, K. (2021, February 18). A killer at 14, his case led to second chances for juvenile murderers: He may soon learn his fate. *AL.com*. www.al.com/news/2021/02/a-killer-at-14-his-case-led-to-second-chances-for-juvenile-murderers-he-may-soon-learn-his-fate.html

Fedders, B. (2010). Losing hold on the guiding hand: Ineffective assistance of counsel in juvenile delinquency representation. *Lewis & Clark Law Review*, *14*, 771–820.

Feeney, F., & Jackson, P. (1991). Public defenders, assigned counsel, retained counsel: Does the type of criminal defense counsel matter. *Rutgers Law Journal*, *22*, 361–456.

Feld, B. C. (1988). *In Re Gault* revisited: A cross- state comparison on the right to counsel in juvenile court. *Crime & Delinquency*, *34*(4), 393–424.

Feld, B. C. (1991). Justice by geography: Urban, suburban, and rural variations in juvenile justice administration. *The Journal of Criminal Law and Criminology, 82*(1), 156–210.

Feld, B. C. (1999). *Bad kids: Race and the transformation of the juvenile court.* Oxford University Press.

Feld, B. C. (2003). The constitutional tension between *Apprendi and McKeiver:* Sentence enhancements based on delinquency convictions and the quality of justice in juvenile courts. *Wake Forest Law Review, 38,* 1111–1224.

Feld, B. C. (2017). *The evolution of the juvenile court: Race, politics and the criminalizing of juvenile justice.* New York University Press.

Fiorillo, S. E. (2013). Mitigating after *Miller*: Legislative consideration and remedied for the future of juvenile sentencing. *Boston University Law Review, 93,* 2095–2129.

Foxhoven, J. R. (2007). Effective assistance of counsel: Quality of representation for juveniles is still illusory. *Barry Law Review, 9,* 99–122.

Friedman, D. R., & Robinson, J. M. (2014). Rebutting the presumption: An empirical analysis of parole deferrals under Marsy's law. *Stanford Law Review, 66,* 173–215.

Glynn, G., & Vila, I. (2012). What states should do to provide a meaningful opportunity for review and release: Recognize human worth and potential. *St. Thomas Law Review, 24,* 310–349.

Goffman, E. (1957). *The presentation of self in everyday life.* Doubleday Publishing.

Goffman, E. (1968). *Stigma: Notes on the management of spoiled identity.* Pelican.

Gonzales, J. (2015). Treating adults like children: Texas juvenile parole hearings and the Texas board of pardons and parole. *Texas Tech Administrative Law Journal, 17,* 107–128.

Griffin, P., Addie, S., Adams, B., & Firestine, K. (2011). *Trying juveniles as adults: An analysis of state transfer laws and reporting.* Juvenile Offenders and Victims: National Report Series. U.S Department of Justice.

Grisso, T. (1997). The competence of adolescents as trial defendants. *Psychology, Public Policy, and Law, 3*(1), 3–32.

Grisso, T. (2017). Assuring the future of developmental reform in juvenile justice: Recommendations of the fourth wave forecasting project. *Models for Change: System Reform in Juvenile Justice.* http://adq631j7v3x1shge52cot6m1-wpengine.netdna-ssl.com/wp-content/uploads/2016/09/Policy_Brief_Assuring_the_Future_of_Developmental_Reform_in_Juvenile_Justice.pdf

Grisso, T., & Kavanaugh, A. (2016). Prospects for developmental evidence in juvenile sentencing based on *Miller v. Alabama. Psychology, Public Policy and Law, 22*(3), 235–249.

Guevara, L., Herz, D., & Spohn, C. (2008). Race, gender, and legal counsel. *Youth Violence and Juvenile Justice, 6*(1), 83–104.

Haas, G., & Magrath, G. (2016). *Parole decisions for lifers: 2016.* Lifers Group Inc.

Hagan, J. (2010). *Who are the criminals? The politics of crime policy from the age of Roosevelt to the age of Reagan.* Princeton University Press.

Harcourt, B. E. (2015). Risk as a proxy for race: The dangers of risk assessment. *Federal Sentencing Reporter, 27*(4), 237–243.

Hartley, R. D., Miller, H. V., & Spohn, C. (2010). Do you get what you pay for? Type of counsel and its effect on criminal court outcomes. *Journal of Criminal Justice, 38*, 1063–1070.

Hawkins, K. (1983). Assessing evil: Decision behavior and parole board justice. *British Journal of Criminology, 23*(2), 101–127.

Hawkins, K. (1986). On legal decision-making. *Washington and Lee Law Review, 43*(4), 1161–1242.

Hier, A. P. (1973). Curbing abuse in the decision to grant or deny parole. *Harvard Civil Rights-Civil Liberties Law Review, 8*(2), 419–468.

Hoesterey, A. R. (2017). Confusion in *Montgomery*'s wake: State responses, the mandates of montgomery, and why a complete categorical ban on life without parole for juveniles is the only constitutional option. *Fordham Urban Law Journal, 45*, 149–199.

Howard, M. M. (2017). *Unusually cruel: Prisons, punishment and the real American exceptionalism*. Oxford University Press.

Hussemann, J., & Siegel, J. (2019). Decision-making and holistic public defense post- *Montgomery v. Louisiana. Criminal Justice Policy Review, 31*(6), 886–907.

Iyengar, R. (2007). *An analysis of the performance of federal indigent defense counsel*. Working Paper 13187. National Bureau of Economic Research. www.ebony.com/wp-content/uploads/2013/08/20070712_indigent_defense.pdf

Jones, J. B. (2004, June). *Access to counsel*. Juvenile Justice Bulletin. OJJDP.

Kempf-Leonard, K. (2010). Does having an attorney provide a better outcome: The right to counsel does not mean attorney help youths juveniles' right to counsel—policy essay. *Criminology & Pub. Policy, 9*, 357–364.

Kinnevy, S., & Caplan, J. M. (2008). *Findings from the AIPI international survey of releasing authorities*. Center for Research on Youth and Social Policy, University of Pennsylvania.

Kokkalera, S. S. (2021). Representing juvenile lifers: Do attorneys in parole hearings matter? *Journal of Crime and Justice*. https://doi.org/10.1080/07356 48X.2021.1918210

Kokkalera, S. S., & Singer, S. I. (2019). Discretionary release practices for juveniles facing life: A review of state parole and resentencing procedures. In C. Spohn & P. Brennan (Eds.), *Handbook on sentencing policies and practices in the 21st century* (Vol. 4, pp. 126–150). Routledge.

Kokkalera, S. S., Tallas, A. M., & Goggin, K. (2021). Contextualizing the impact of legal representation on juvenile court outcomes: A review of research and policy. *The Juvenile and Family Court Journal, 72*(1), 47–71.

Lavin-Loucks, D., & Levan, K. (2015). "Were you drunk at the time?": The influence of parole boards on accounts and neutralization techniques in state parole hearings. *Journal of Qualitative Criminal Justice and Criminology, 3*(1), 1–27.

Lavin-Loucks, D., & Levan, K. (2018). Identity, discourse and rehabilitation in parole hearings in the United States. *Journal of Prison Education & Reentry, 5*(1), 18–40.

Levick, M. L., & Schwartz, R. G. (2013). Practical implications of *Miller v Jackson*: Obtaining relief in court and before the parole board. *Law & Inequality, 31*, 369–409.

Lin, J., Grattet, R., & Petersilia, J. (2012). Justice by other means: Venue sorting in parole revocation. *Law and Policy, 34*(4), 349–372.

Lynch, M. (2016). *Hard bargains: The coercive power of drug laws in federal court.* Russell Sage Foundation.

Lynch, M. (2017). The situated actor and the production of punishment: Toward an empirical social psychology of criminal procedure. In S. Dolovich & A. Natapoff (Eds.), *The new criminal justice thinking* (pp. 199–225). New York University Press.

Maier, E. A. (2009). Juvenile court variations: Procedural and processing differences in a midwestern state. *Juvenile and Family Court Journal, 60*, 37–54.

Marquez-Lewis, C., Fine, M., Boudin, K., Waters, W. E., DeVeaux, M., Vargas, F., & White-Harrigan, S. (2013). How much punishment is enough? Designing participatory research on parole policies for persons convicted for violent crimes. *Journal of Social Issues, 69*(4), 771–796.

Marshall, M. (2019). *Miller v. Alabama* and the problem of prediction. *Columbia Law Review, 119*, 1633–1669.

Martel, J. (2010). Remorse and the production of truth. *Punishment and Society, 12*(4), 414–437.

McCafferty, J. T., & Travis, L. F. (2014). History of probation and parole in the United States. In G. Bruinsma & D. Weisburd (Eds.), *Encyclopedia of criminology and criminal justice* (pp. 2217–2227). Springer.

Mears, D. P., & Travis, J. (2004). Youth development and reentry. *Youth Violence and Juvenile Justice, 2*, 3–20.

Medwed, D. (2008). The innocent prisoner's dilemma: Consequences of failing to admit guilt at parole hearings. *Iowa Law Review, 93*, 491–557.

Miles, M. B., Huberman, M. A., & Saldana, J. (2014). *Qualitative data analysis: A methods sourcebook.* Sage Publications Inc.

Mlyenic, W. J. (2008). *In Re Gault* at 40: The right to counsel in juvenile court- a promise unfulfilled. *Criminal Law Bulletin, 44*(3), 371–412.

Morgan, K. D., & Smith, B. (2005). Parole release decisions revisited: An analysis of parole release decisions for violent inmates in a southeastern state. *Journal of Criminal Justice, 33*(3), 277–287.

Moriearty, P. L. (2017a). The trilogy and beyond. *South Dakota Law Review, 62*, 539–558.

Moriearty, P. L. (2017b). Implementing proportionality. *U.C. Davis Law Review, 50*, 961–1028.

Mulvey, E., & Schubert, C. A. (2012a, December). Transfer of juveniles to adult court: Effects of a broad policy in one court. *Juvenile Justice Bulletin*, 1–17.

Mulvey, E., & Schubert, C. A. (2012b). Youth in prison and beyond. In B. C. Feld & D. Bishop (Eds.), *The Oxford handbook of juvenile crime and juvenile justice* (pp. 843–870). Oxford University Press.

National Juvenile Defender Center (NJDC). (2017). *Access denied: A national snapshot of states' failure to protect children's right to counsel.* NJDC.

National Juvenile Defender Center (NJDC). (2019). *Role of counsel/scope of representation.* https://njdc.info/role-of-counsel/

Naughton, C., O'Donnell, A. T., Greenwood, R. M., & Muldoon, O. T. (2015). Ordinary decent domestic violence: A Discursive Analysis of family law judges' interview. *Discourse & Society, 26*(3), 349–365.

Nellis, A. (2012). *The lives of juvenile lifers: Findings from a national survey.* The Sentencing Project.

Nellis, A., & King, R. S. (2009). *No exit: The expanding use of life sentences in America.* The Sentencing Project.

Newman, D. J. (1972). Court intervention in the parole process. *Albany Law Review, 36,* 257–304.

Nuffield, J. (1982). *Parole decision-making in Canada: Research towards decision guidelines.* Minister of Supply and Services.

Ortega, B. (2015). Introduction to the 2015 Robert D'Agostino symposium edition of the John Marshall law journal: Decreasing youth incarceration through quality juvenile defense. *John Marshall Law Journal, 8*(2), 287–309.

Palacios, V. J. (1994). Go and sin no more: Rationality and release decisions by parole boards. *South Carolina Law Review, 45,* 567–616.

Peck, J. H., & Beaudry-Cyr, M. (2016). Does who appears before the juvenile court matter on adjudication and disposition outcomes? The interaction between client race and lawyer type. *Journal of Crime and Justice, 39*(1), 131–152.

Potter, J., & Wetherell, N. (1987). *Discourse and social Psychology: Beyond attitudes and behavior.* Sage Publications Inc.

Primus, E. B. (2007). Structural reform in criminal defense: Relocating ineffective assistance of counsel claims. *Cornell Law Review, 92,* 679–732.

Proctor, J. L. (1999). The "new parole": An analysis of parole board decision making as a function of eligibility. *Journal of Crime and Justice, 22*(2), 193–217.

Radelet, M. L., & Roberts, L. M. (1983). Parole interviews of sex offenders: The role of impression management. *Urban Life, 12*(2), 140–161.

Reitz, K., & Rhine, E. E. (2020). Parole release and supervision: Critical drivers of American prison policy. *Annual Review of Criminology, 3,* 281–298.

Rhine, E. E. (2012). The present status and future prospects of parole boards and parole supervisions. In J. Petersilia & K. R. Reitz (Eds.), *The Oxford handbook of sentencing and corrections* (pp. 627–656). Oxford University Press.

Rossmanith, K. (2013). Getting into the box: Risky enactments of remorse in the courtroom. *About Performance, 12,* 7–26.

Rovner, J. (2014). *Slow to act: State responses to 2012 court mandate on life without parole.* The Sentencing Project.

Rovner, J. (2016). *How tough on crime became tough on kids: Prosecuting teenage drug charges in adult court.* The Sentencing Project.

Rovner, J. (2017). *Juvenile life without parole: An overview.* The Sentencing Project.

Rovner, J. (2021). *Juvenile life without parole: An overview.* The Sentencing Project.

Ruhland, E. L., Rhine, E. E., Robey, J. P., & Mitchell, K. L. (2017). *The continuing leverage of release authorities: Findings from a national survey.* Robina Institute of Criminal Law and Criminal Justice, University of Minnesota.

Russell, S. F. (2014). Review for release: Juvenile Offenders, state parole practices and the eighth amendment. *Indiana Law Journal, 89,* 373–440.

Russell, S. F. (2016). The role of crime at juvenile parole hearings: A response to Beth Caldwell's *creating meaningful opportunities for release*. *The Harbinger*, *41*, 227–232.

Scholssman, S. L. (1977). *Love and the American delinquent: The theory and practice of "progressive" juvenile justice, 1825–1920*. University of Chicago Press.

Schwartzapfel, B. (2015, July 11). How parole boards keep prisoners in the dark and behind bars. *The Washington Post*. www.washingtonpost.com/national/the-power-and-politics-of-parole-boards/2015/07/10/49c1844e-1f71-11e5-84d5-eb37ee8eaa61_story.html?utm_term=.d2b72a26e74d

Scott, E., Grisso, T., Levick, M., & Steinberg, L. (2015). *The supreme court and the transformation of juvenile sentencing*. Models for Change: System Reforms in Juvenile Justice.

Scott, E., & Steinberg, L. (2008). *Rethinking juvenile justice*. Harvard University Press.

Seale, C. (Ed.). (2012). *Researching society and culture* (3rd ed.). Sage Publications Inc.

Seeds, C. (2018). Disaggregating LWOP: Life without parole, capital punishment and mass incarceration in Florida, 1972–1995. *Law & Society Review*, *52*(1), 172–205.

Simkins, S., & Cohen, L. (2015). The critical role of post-disposition representation in addressing the needs of incarcerated youth. *John Marshall Law Journal*, *8*(2), 311–402.

Simon, J. (2007). *Governing through crime: How the war on crime transformed American democracy and created a culture of fear*. Oxford University Press.

Singer, S. I. (1996). *Recriminalizing delinquency: Violent juvenile crime and juvenile justice reform*. Cambridge University Press.

Singer, S. I. (2017, October 16). Parole boards treat adolescents who grow up in prisons like adults-and that's wrong. *Juvenile Justice Information Exchange*. http://jjie.org/2017/10/16/parole-boards-treat-adolescents-who-grow-up-in-prison-like-adults-and-thats-wrong/

Singer, S. S., & Kokkalera, S. S. (Forthcoming). Contemporizing the social organization of parole: A critical assessment. In M. Godwyn (Ed.), *The research handbook on the sociology of organizations*. Edward Edgar Publishing.

Stapleton, V. V., & Teitelbaum, L. E. (1972). *In defense of youth: A study of the role of counsel in American juvenile courts*. Russell Sage Foundation.

Starks, H., & Trinidad, S. B. (2007). Choose your method: A comparison of phenomenology, discourse analysis, and grounded theory. *Qualitative Health Research*, *17*, 1372–1380.

Steinberg, L. D. (2014). *Age of opportunity: Lessons from the new science of adolescence*. Eamon Dolan, Houghton Mifflin Harcourt.

Talbot, K. M., & Quayle, M. (2010). The perils of being a nice guy: Contextual variation in five young women's constructions of acceptable hegemonic and alternative masculinities. *Men and Masculinities*, *13*(2), 255–278.

Thomas, K., & Reingold, P. (2017). From grace to grids: Rethinking due process protection for parole. *The Journal of Criminal Law and Criminology*, *107*(2), 213–252.

Tobey, A., Grisso, T., & Schwartz, R. (2000). Youths' trial participation as seen by youths and their attorneys: An exploration of competence-based issues. In T. Grisso & R. Schwartz (Eds.), *Youth on trial: A developmental perspective on juvenile justice* (pp. 225–242). University of Chicago Press.

Tonkiss, F. (2012). Discourse analysis. In C. Seale (Ed.), *Researching society and culture* (3rd ed., pp. 405–423). Sage Publications Inc.

Tonry, M. H. (2019). Fifty years of American sentencing reform: Nine lessons. *Crime and Justice, 48*, 1–34.

Trahos, P. (2016). From homicidal youths to reformed adults: Parole hearing procedures for juvenile homicide offenders in *Diatchenko v. District Attorney for Suffolk District. Boston College Journal of Law and Social Justice, 36*(3), 52–63.

Trounstine, J. (2016). *Boy with a knife- a story of murder, remorse and a prisoner's fight for justice.* IG Publishing.

Viljoen, J. L., & Wingrove, T. (2007). Adjudicative competence in adolescent defendants: Judges' and defense attorneys' views of legal standard for adolescents in juvenile and criminal court. *Psychology, Public Policy, and Law, 13*(3), 204–229.

Weingraf, T. (2001). *Qualitative research interviewing: Biographic narrative and semi- structured methods.* Rowman & Littlefield Publishers, Inc.

Wells, K. (2011). *Narrative inquiry.* Pocket Guides to Social Work Research Methods. Oxford University Press.

Williams, M. R. (2002). A comparison of sentencing outcomes for defendants with public defenders versus retained counsel in a Florida circuit court. *Justice System Journal, 23*(2), 249–257.

Williams, M. R. (2013). The effectiveness of public defenders in four Florida counties. *Journal of Criminal Justice, 41*, 205–212.

Willig, C. (2014). Discourses and discourse analysis. In U. Flick (Ed.), *The Sage handbook of qualitative data analysis* (pp. 341–353). Sage Publications Inc.

Wills, C. D. (2017). Right to counsel in juvenile court 50 years after *In Re Gault. The Journal of the Academy of Psychiatry and the Law, 45*, 140–144.

Witmer, H. L. (1925). Some factors in success or failure on parole. *Journal of Criminal Law & Criminology, 18*, 384–403.

Witmer, H. L. (1927). The development of parole in the United States. *Social Forces, 4*(2), 318–325.

Zane, S. N., Singer, S. I., & Welsh, B. C. (2021). The right to a good defense: Investigating the influence of attorney type across urban counties for juveniles in criminal court. *Criminal Justice Policy Review, 32*(2), 162–192.

Zimring, F. E. (2000). The common thread: Diversion in juvenile justice. *California Law Review, 88*(6), 2477–2495.

Zimring, F. E. (2005). *American juvenile justice.* Oxford University Press.

Zimring, F. E. (2010). The power politics of juvenile court transfer: A mildly revisionist history of the 1990s. *Louisiana Law Review, 71*, 1–15.

Zucker, B. (2005). Triumph for *Gideon*: The evolution of the right to counsel for California parolees in parole revocation proceedings. *Western State University Law Review, 33*(1–2), 1–12.

# Index

Note: Page numbers in **bold** indicate a table and page numbers followed by an "n" indicate a note on the corresponding page.

www.ingramcontent.com/pod-product-compliance
Ingram Content Group UK Ltd.
Pitfield, Milton Keynes, MK11 3LW, UK
UKHW020426010325
455677UK00029B/1027